Copyright © 2021 by JR Reyes.
All rights reserved.
All images by the author unless otherwise noted.

ISBN: 9798531349583
Independently published

No part of this publication may be reproduced, stored, or transmitted in any form or by any means, electronic, mechanical, photocopied, recorded or otherwise, without prior written consent from author.

NOTICE OF DISCLAIMER: the information contained in this book is based on the author's experience and opinions. The author and publisher will not be held liable for the use, mis use or misinterpretation of the information in this book.

CONTENTS

ABOUT THE AUTHOR 4

PREFACE 6

LAST WORDS 35

MODELS (INDEX) 38

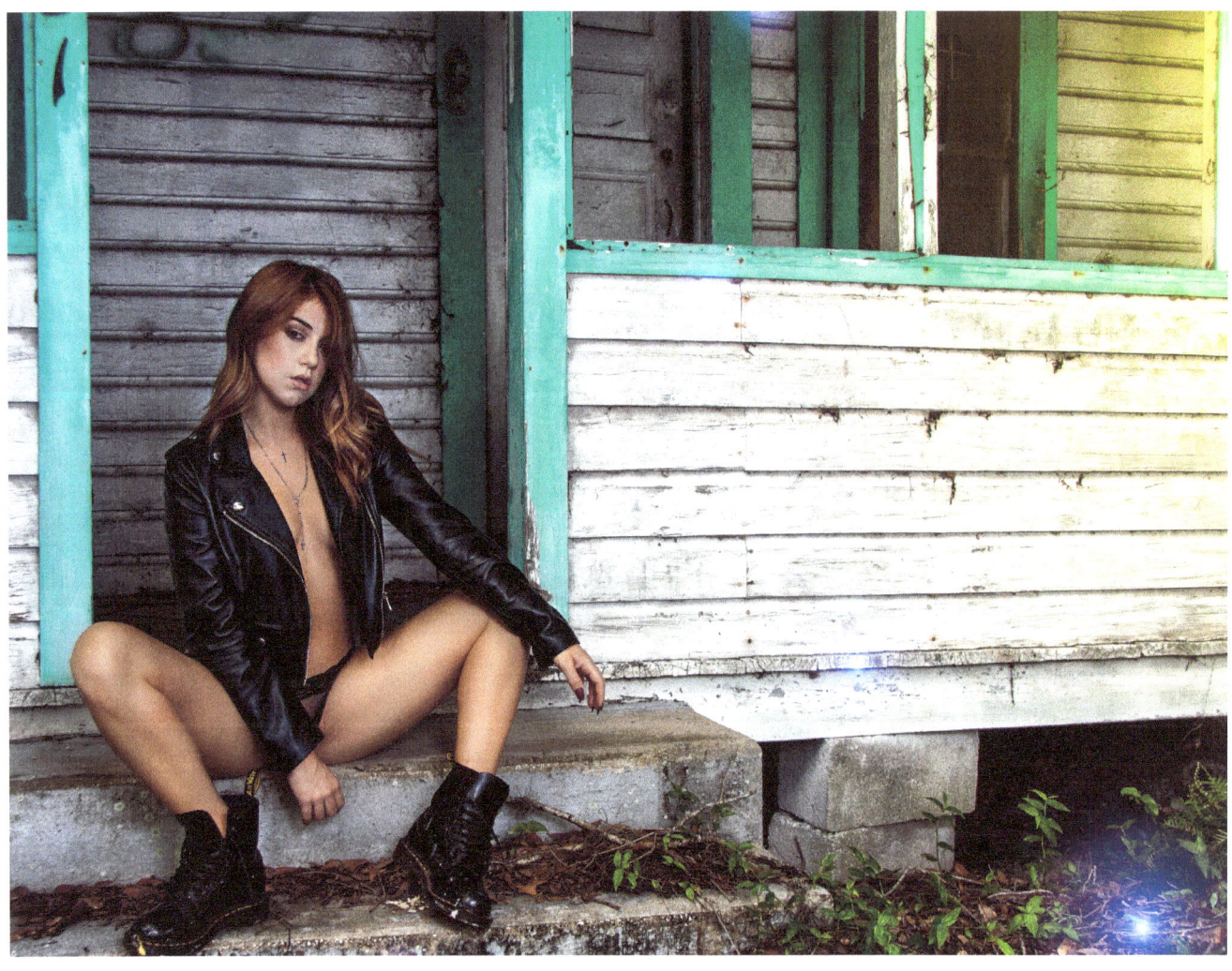

"Good art is art that allows you to enter it from a variety of angles and to emerge with a variety of views"

- Mary Schmich, American - Journalist

About the Author

This is the part of the booklet where I talk about myself. I will be brief. This is a photo booklet, not a textbook.

Who is JR Reyes?

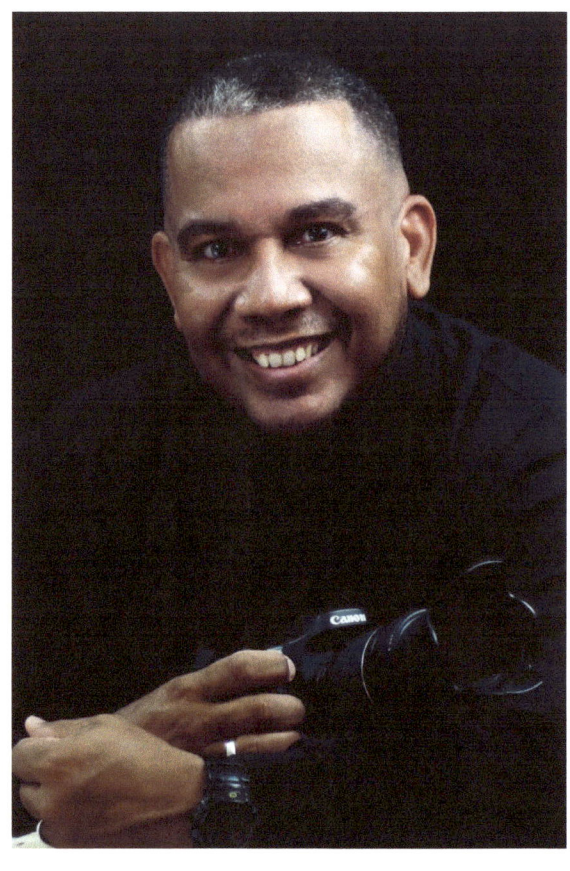

Born and raised in PR. My interest in photography started at an early age long before the era of digital photography. I would take my uncle's camera, whatever he had, and use it as if it was mine, hiding from him of course. In those days all cameras were film cameras. I spent all my money, and part of my mom's money, on photo processing. For a teenager from a poor family this hobby was very expensive. Polaroid Instant Camera technology was also expensive. I dreamed of having a dark room so that I could develop my photos. I never had it because, thanks to God, the era of digital photos began.

As it always happens in life, priorities change. Hobbies take second or third place. Photography became an occasional thing.

I became a parent even as a teenager right after high school. I immediately joined the United States Army. At the end of my military service, I returned to Puerto Rico and enrolled in the State University. I earned a bachelor's degree in business administration thanks to the GI Bill college tuition benefits from the U.S. Armed Forces. It was after that that I rediscovered my passion for photography when working as an assistant manager in a multinational office and school supply store chain. There I also found a new passion: Adobe Photoshop and graphic design.

I quickly became a Photoshop fan, totally obsessed with learning the full power of this computer program. To this day I continue to be a perennial Photoshop learner and a total addict to this amazing software. I describe myself as a graphic artist and not as a photographer. Photography is now not the passion that defines me but rather the vehicle that leads me to my new passion: photo editing and graphic design.

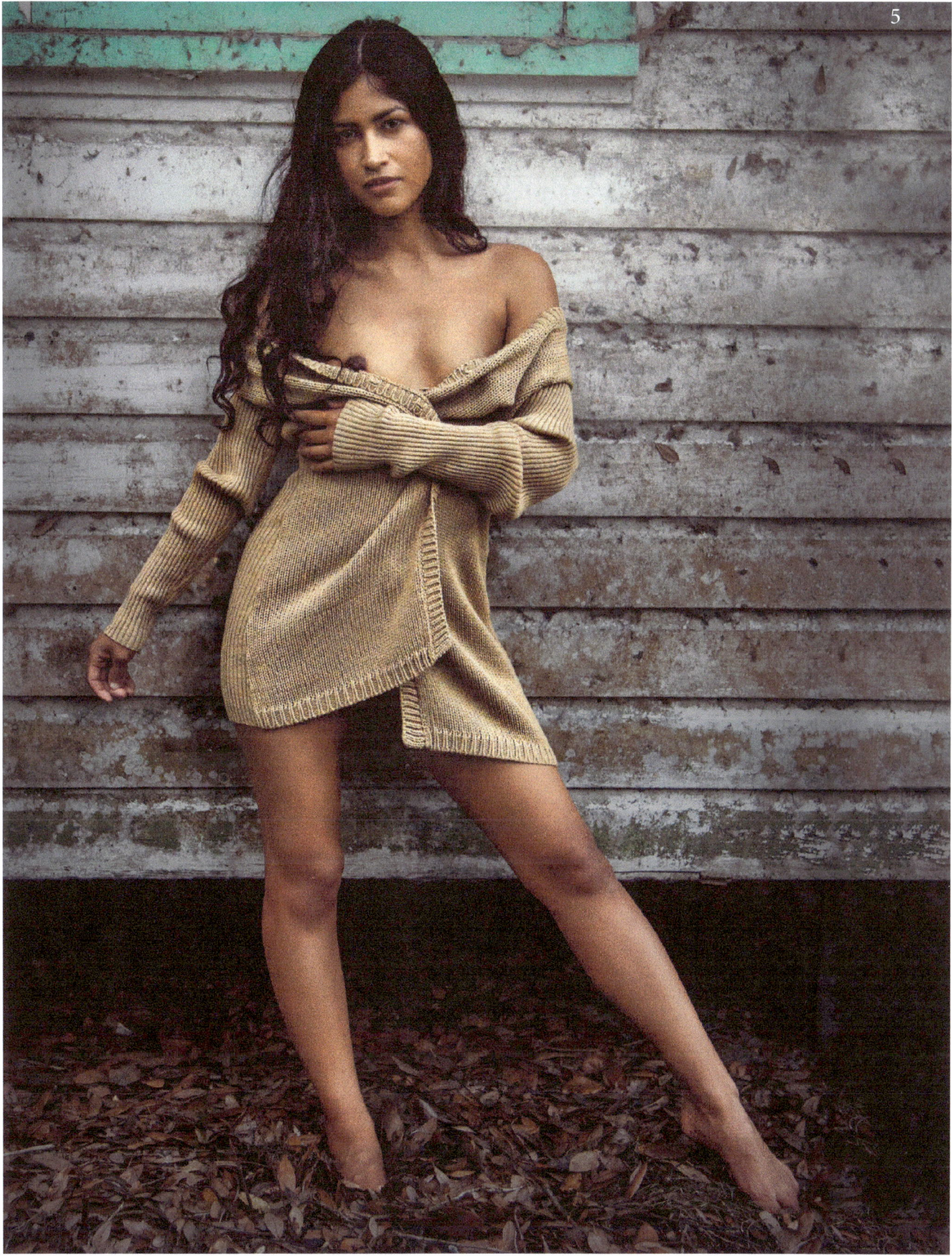

Preface

Photo shooting in abandoned places arose more out of necessity than creativity. Before buying my house, I had a small photography studio, in my small two bedroom apartment, that I used to create the material I needed to publish my magazines. A family tragedy occurred. It forced my wife and I to bring and absorb two family members of hers into our home. My photography studio became a bedroom. To continue publishing the modeling magazines that I have published since 2015, I had no other choice but to do outdoor photography.

Little by little I began to be drawn to the abandoned places close to where I live. Lonely buildings full of silence and traces of a past unknown to me. The beauty of the abandoned has an attractive magic that is what led me more and more to seek these rural corners in decay. There is something forbidden (a lot, in fact) when entering an abandoned place. A certain fear that is mixed with a spirit of adventure and with our feeling of anxiety or discomfort about absolute silence. A special silence that only comes out of a place where there has been no one for years, decades perhaps, and the only life that sprouts is the vegetation that grows uncontrollably everywhere.

I had the idea of contrasting the decadence of these sites with the beauty of the models that I photographed for my magazines. I found myself searching for more and more abandoned places to photograph. In the same way, surprisingly, I also found more and more adventurous enough models to explore these places with.

This publication is not a study of techniques and forms, it is a collection of photos of beautiful models in decrepit places. This photo booklet is the result of several years of doing photography in abandoned places.

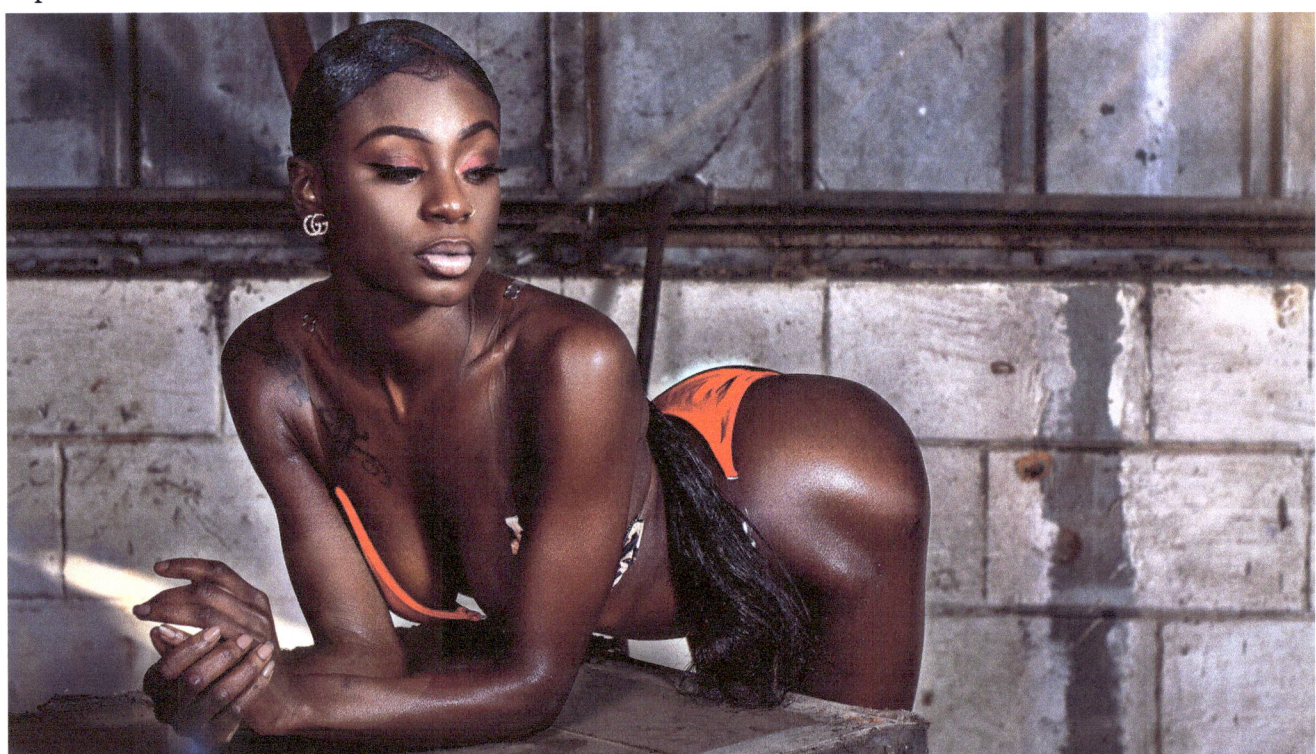

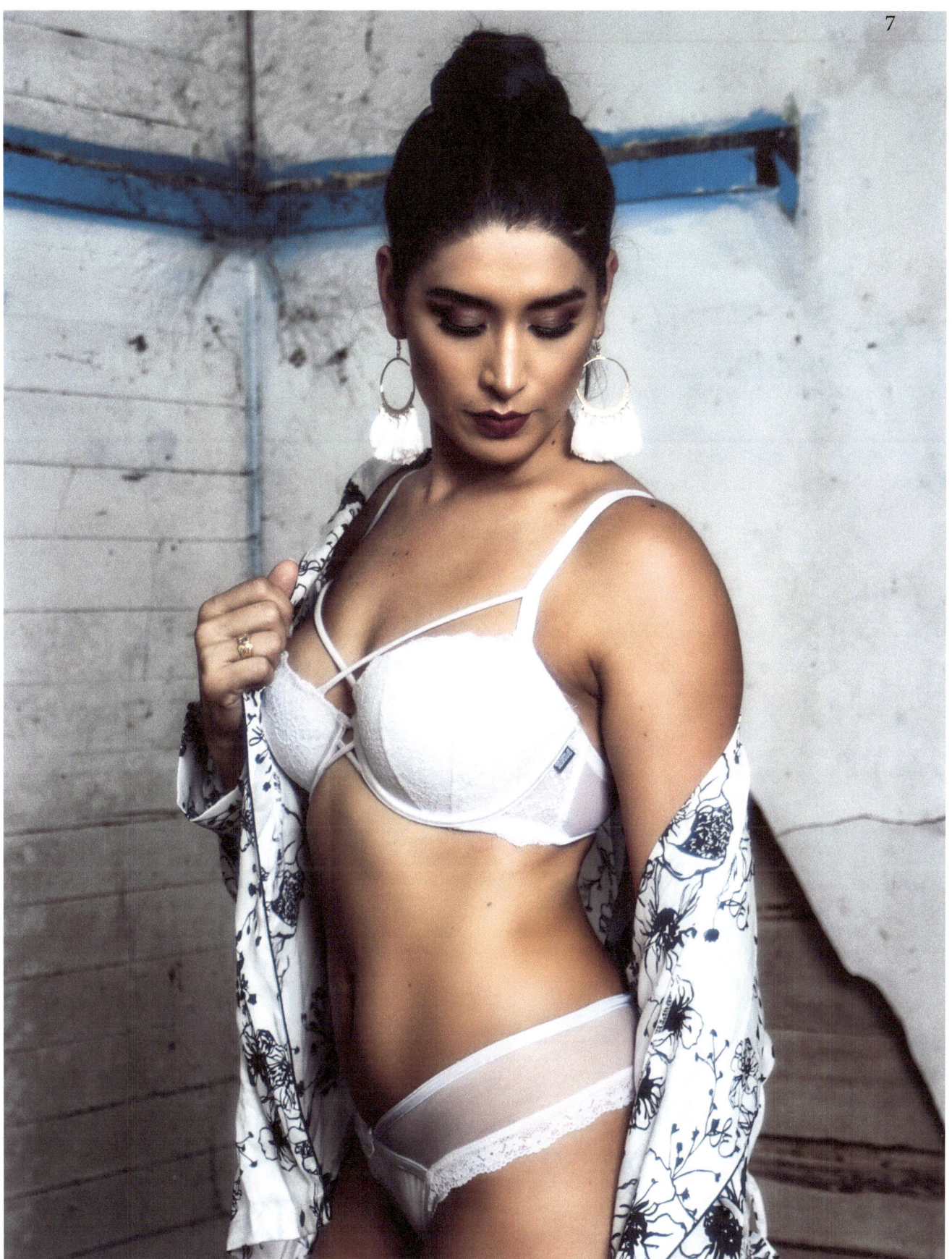

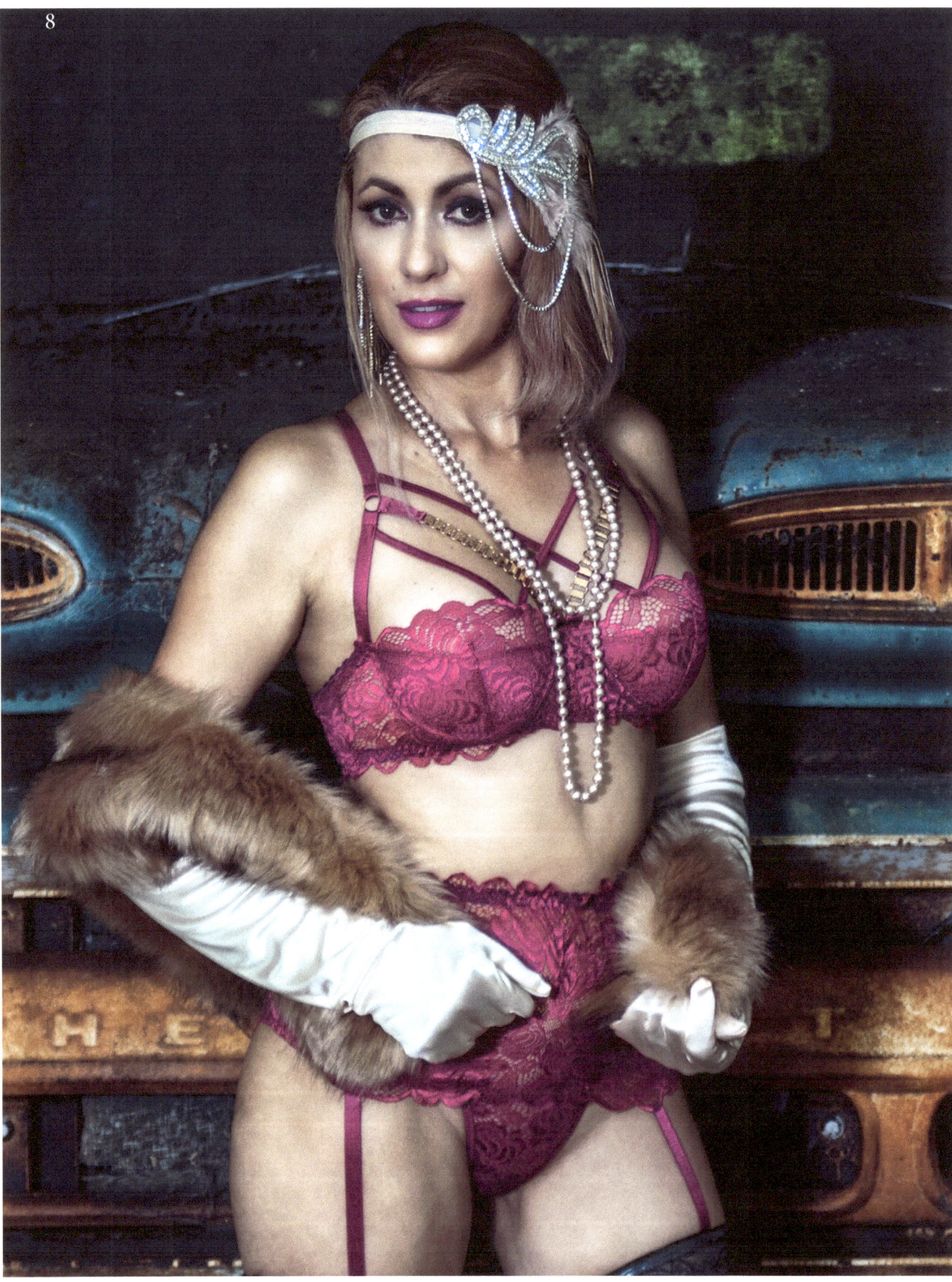

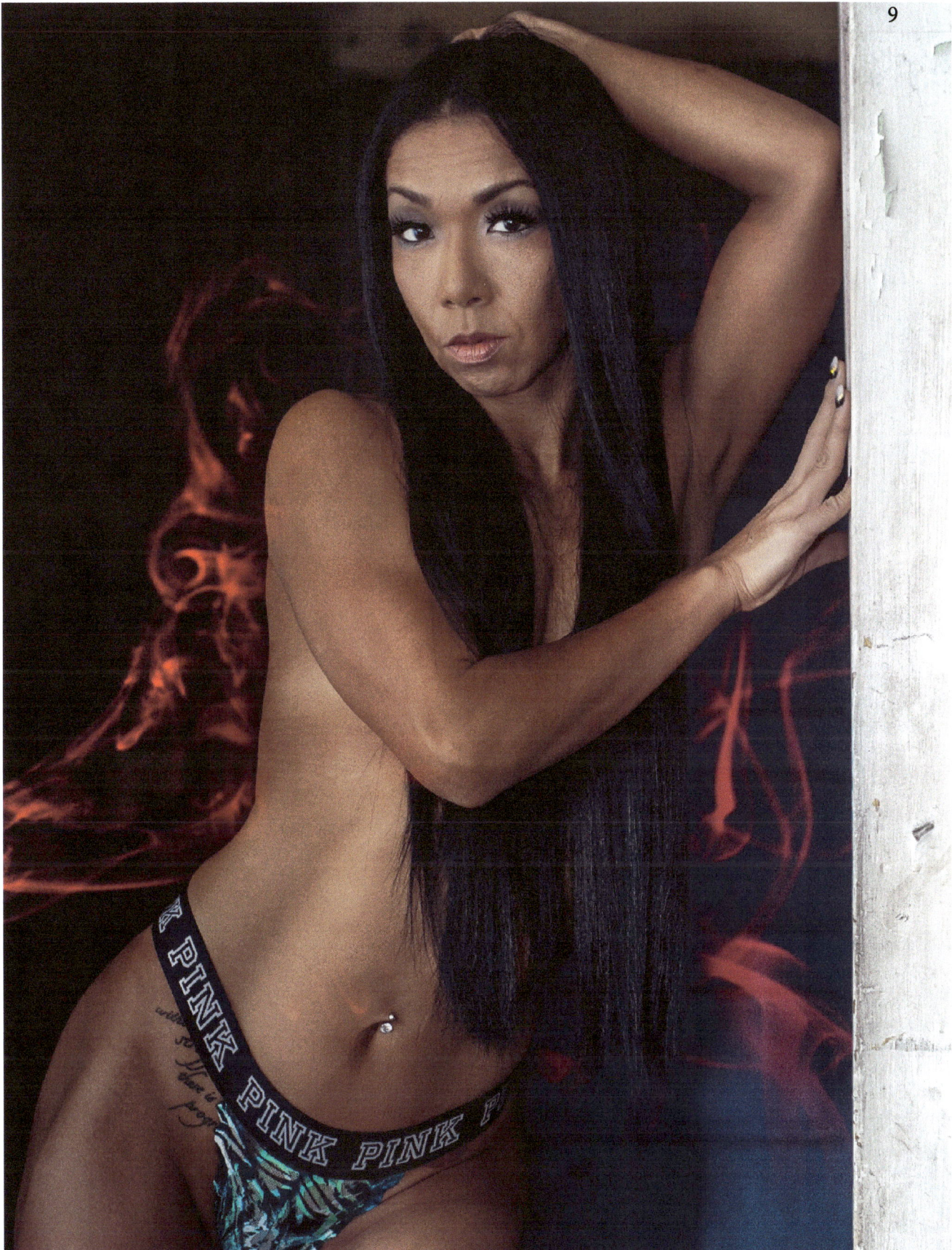

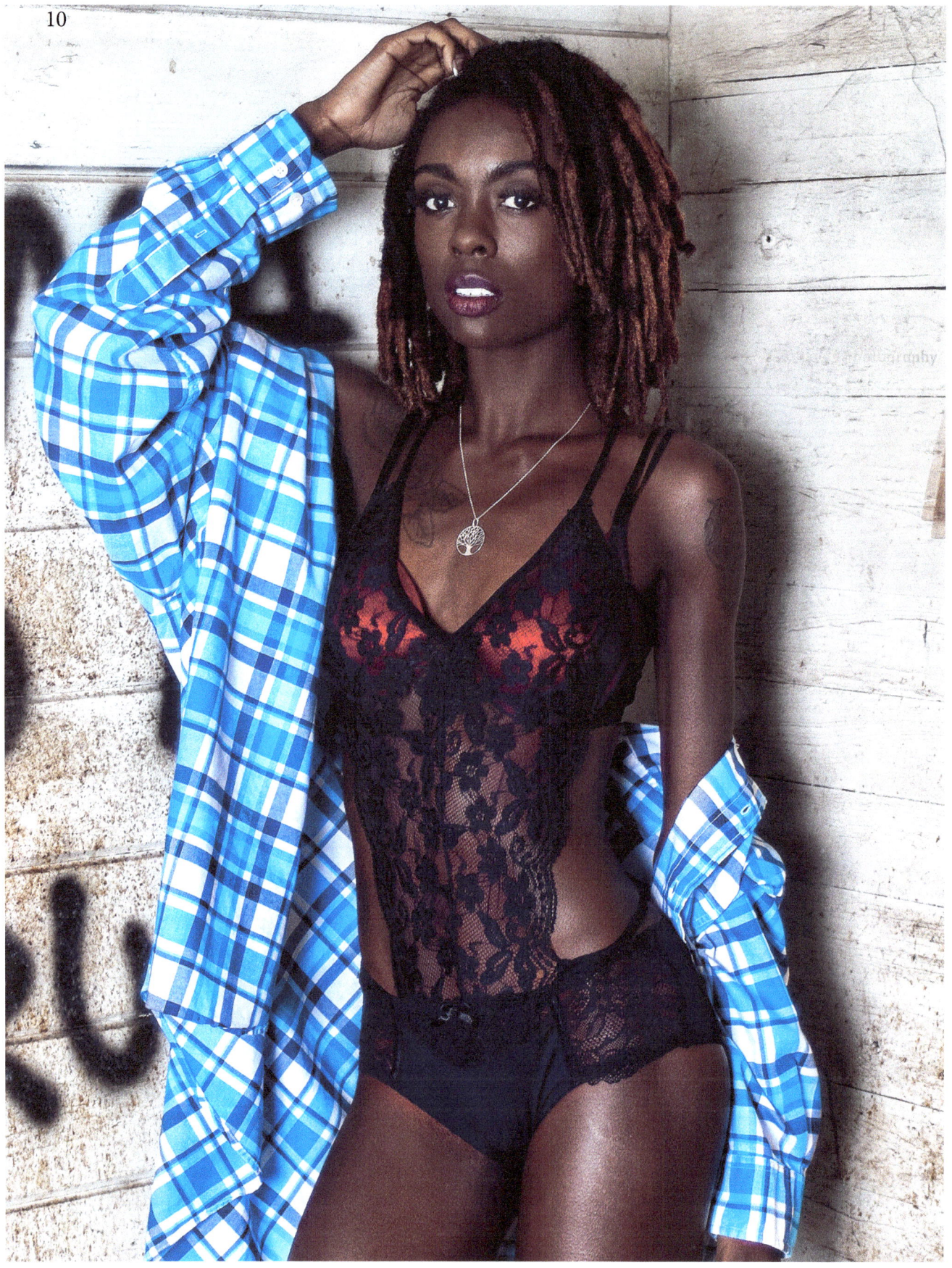

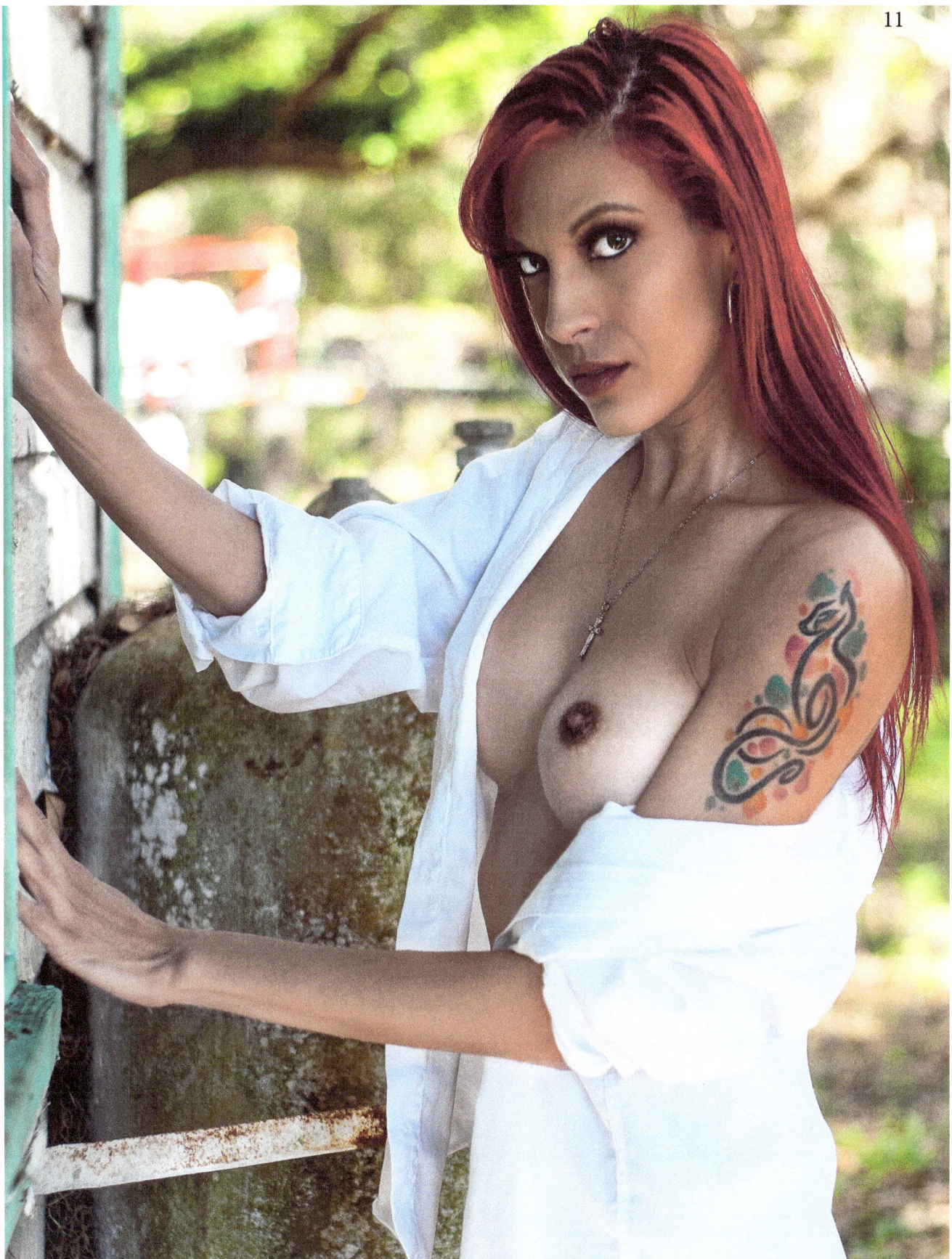

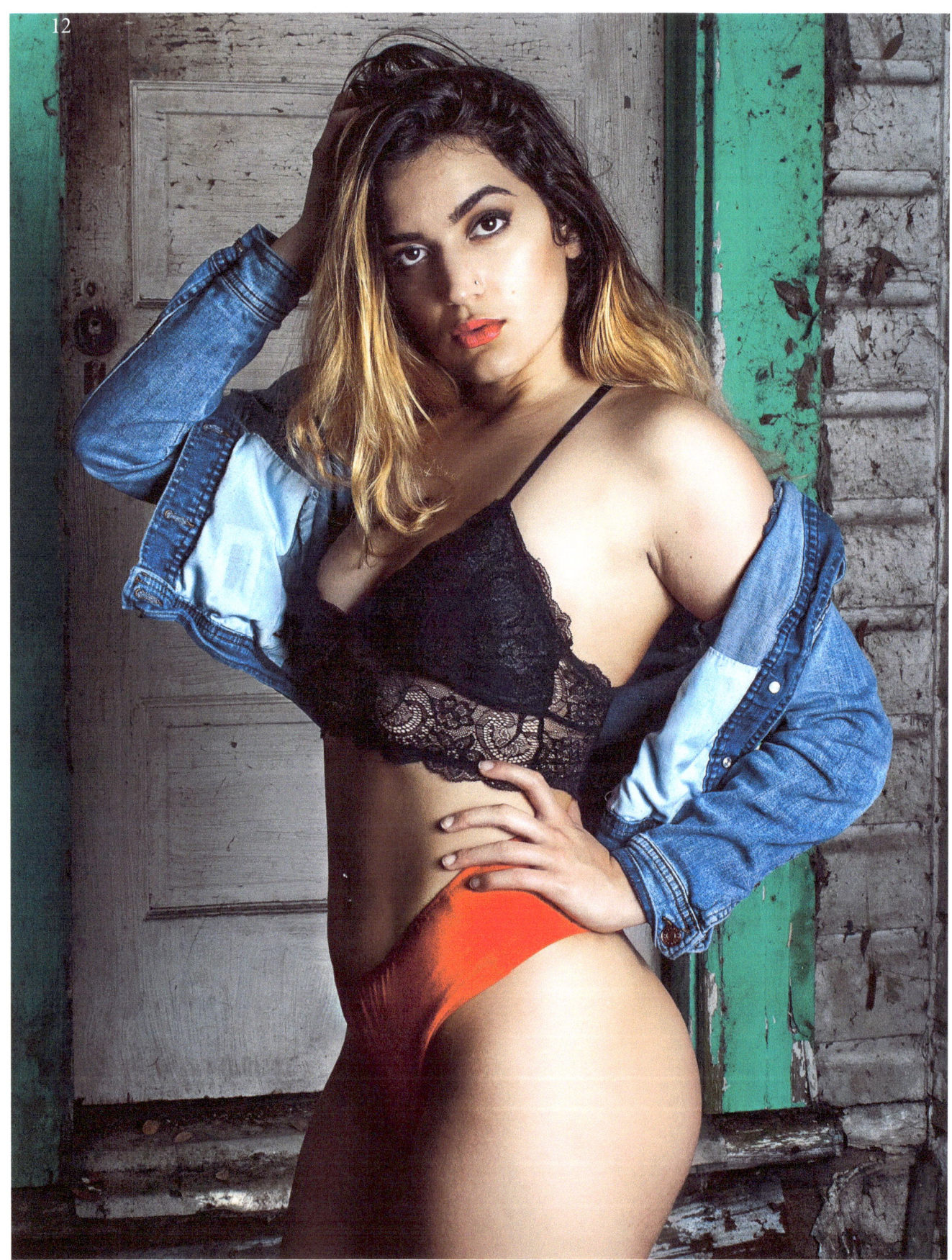

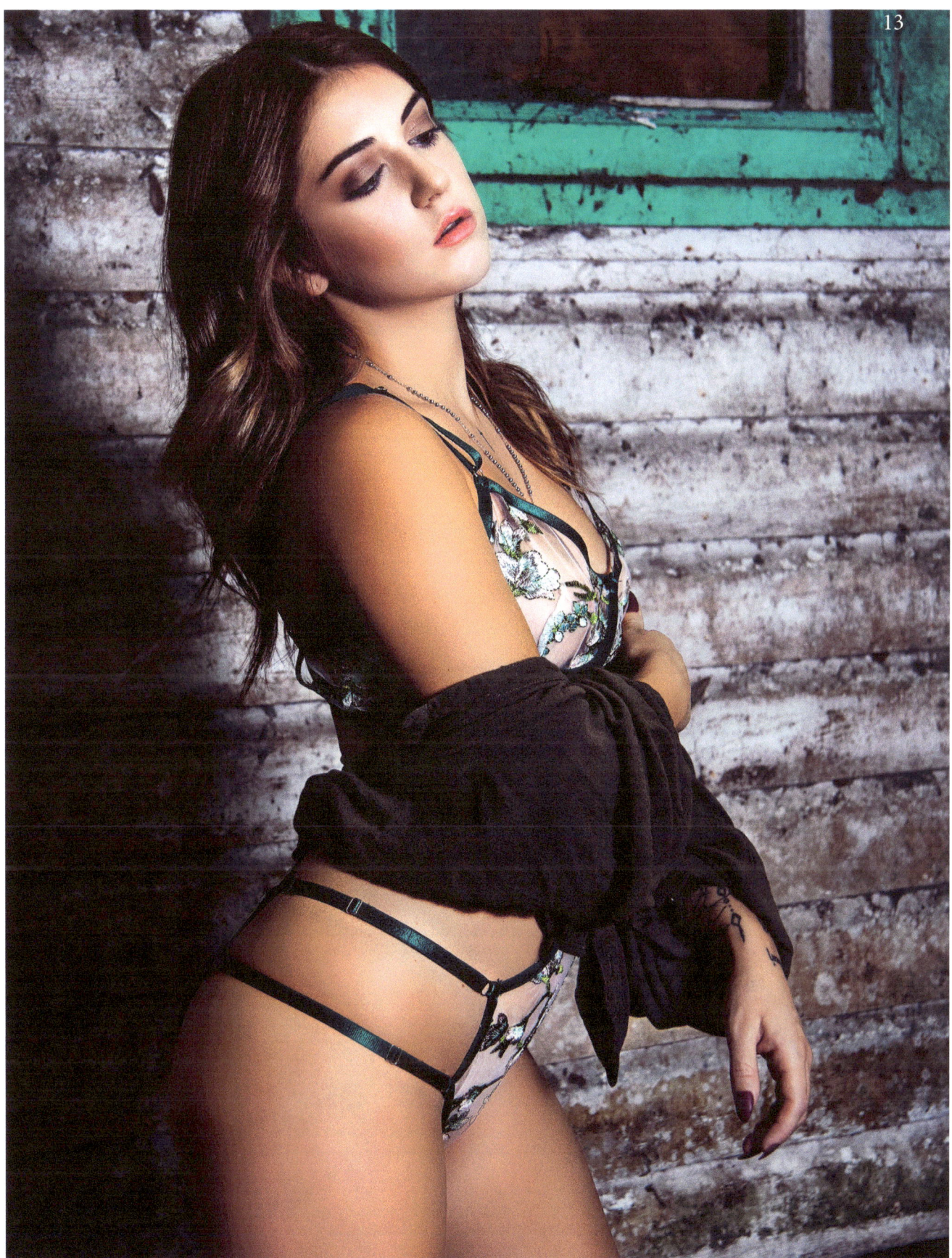

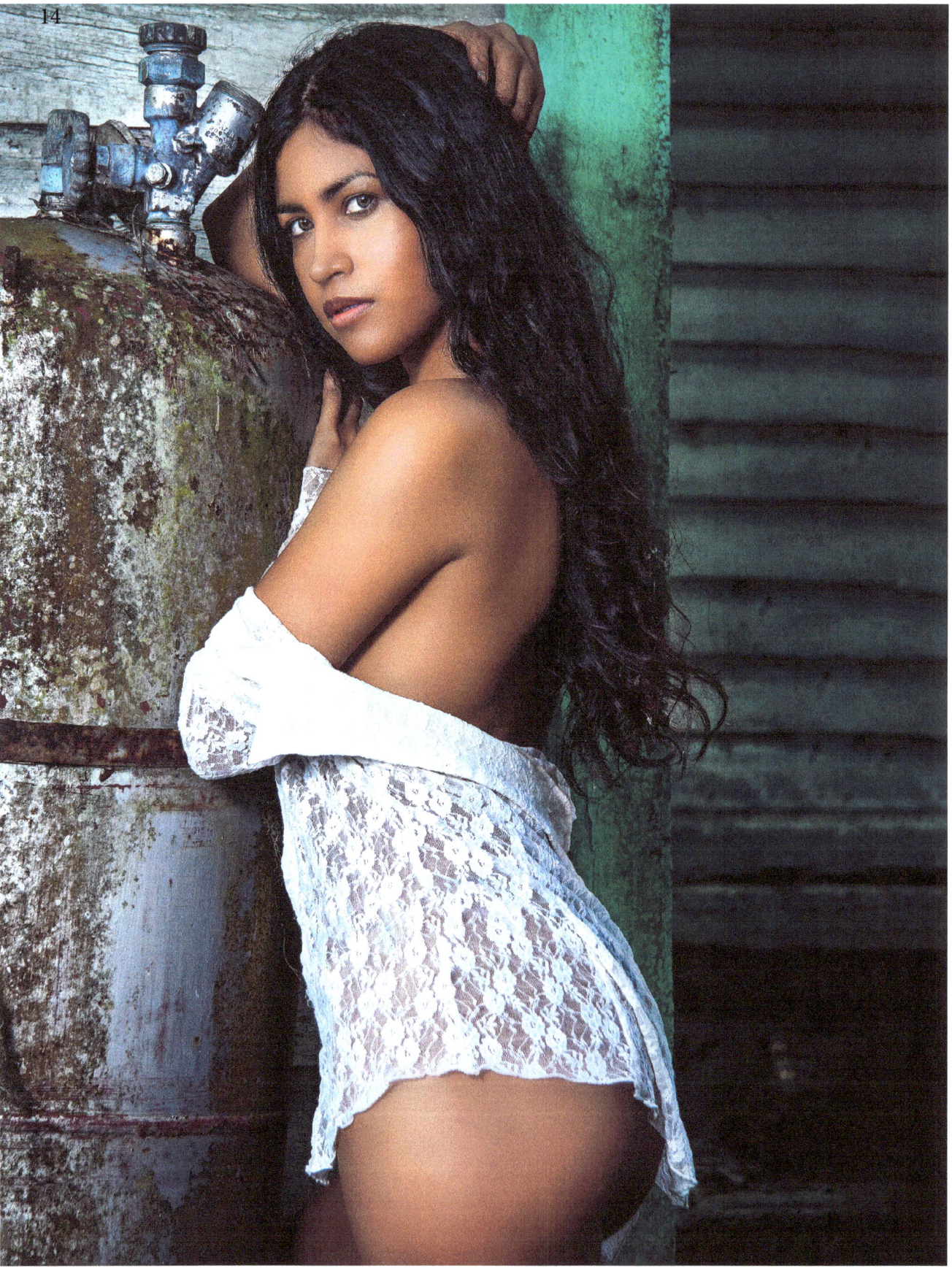

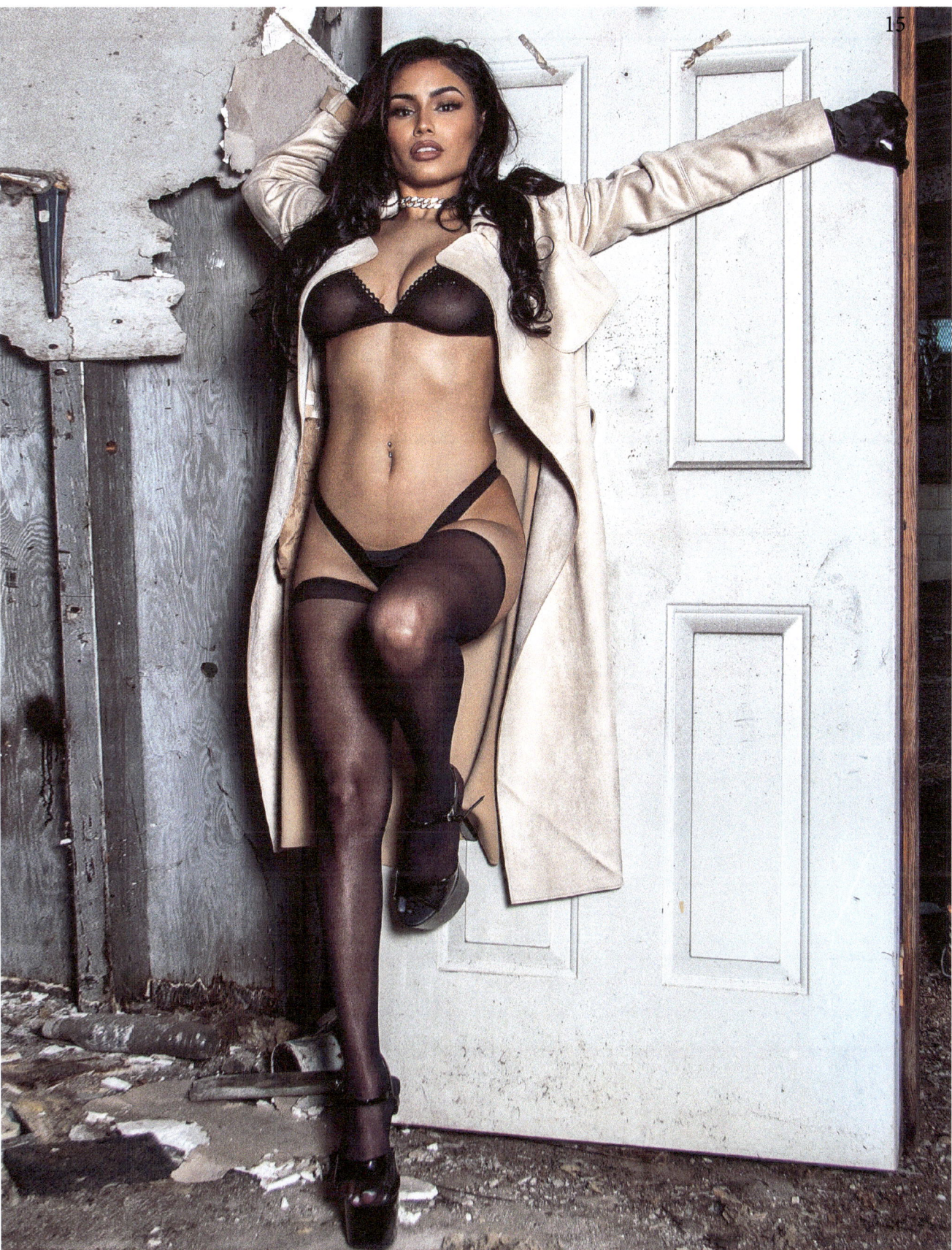

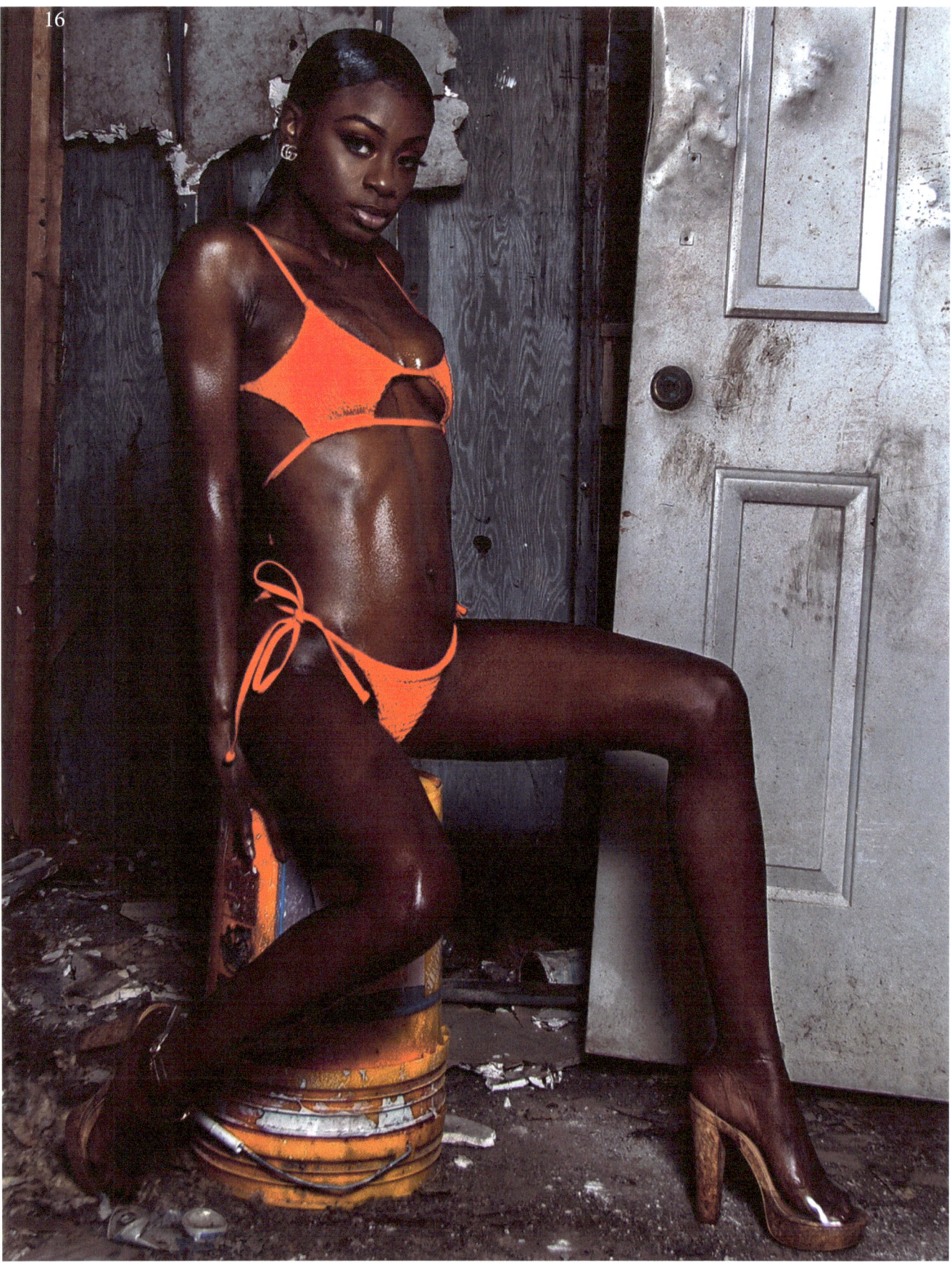

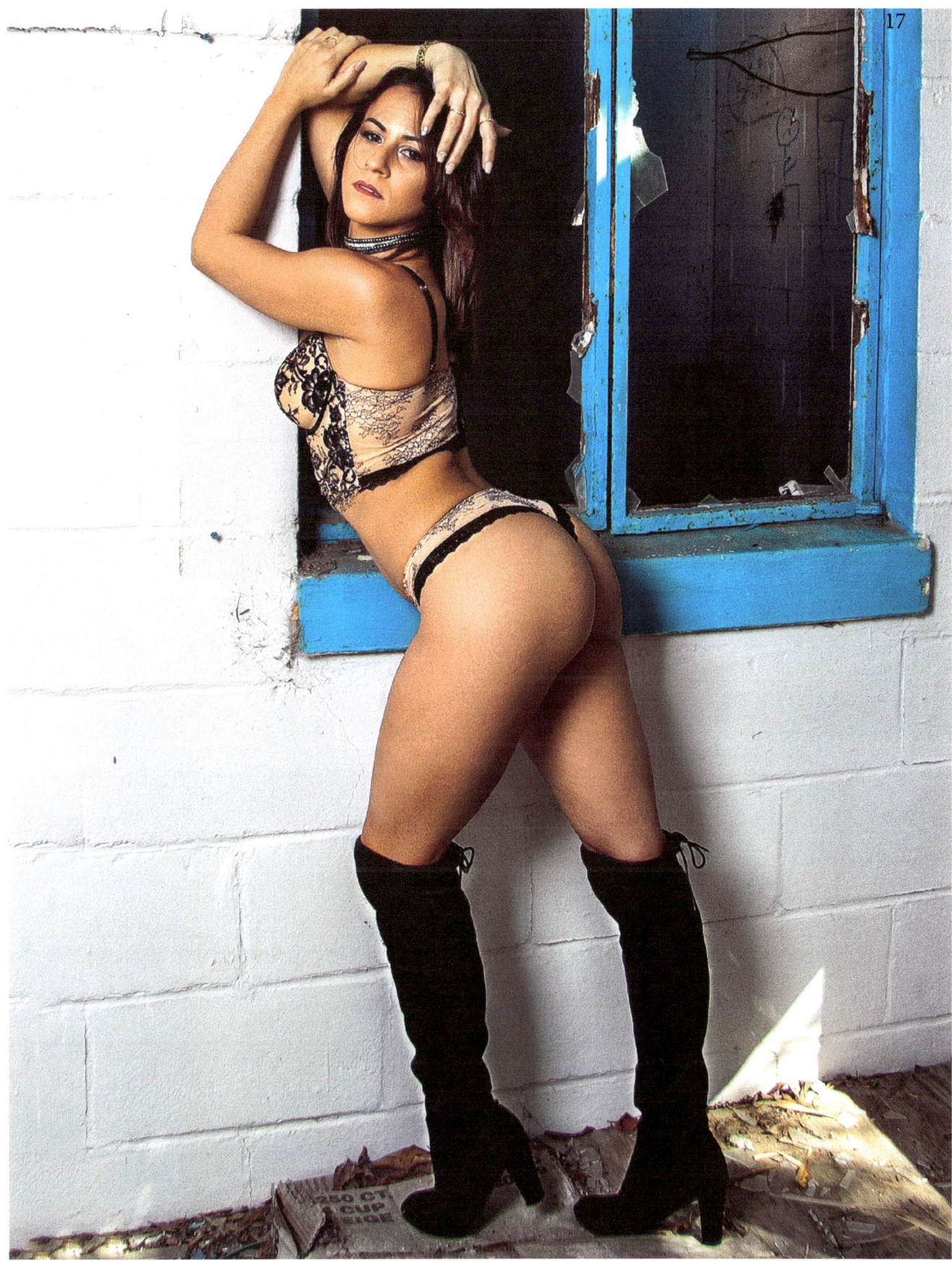

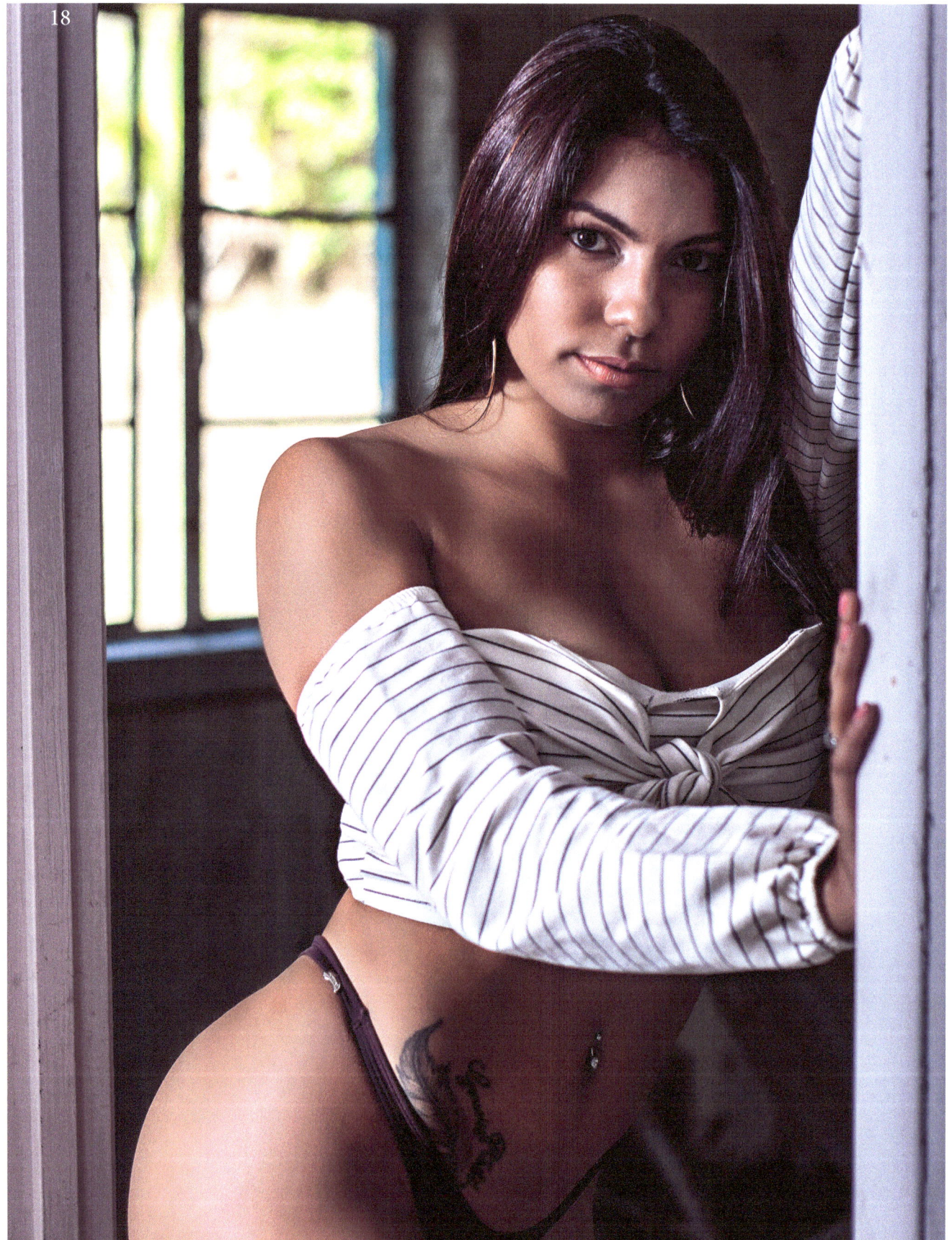

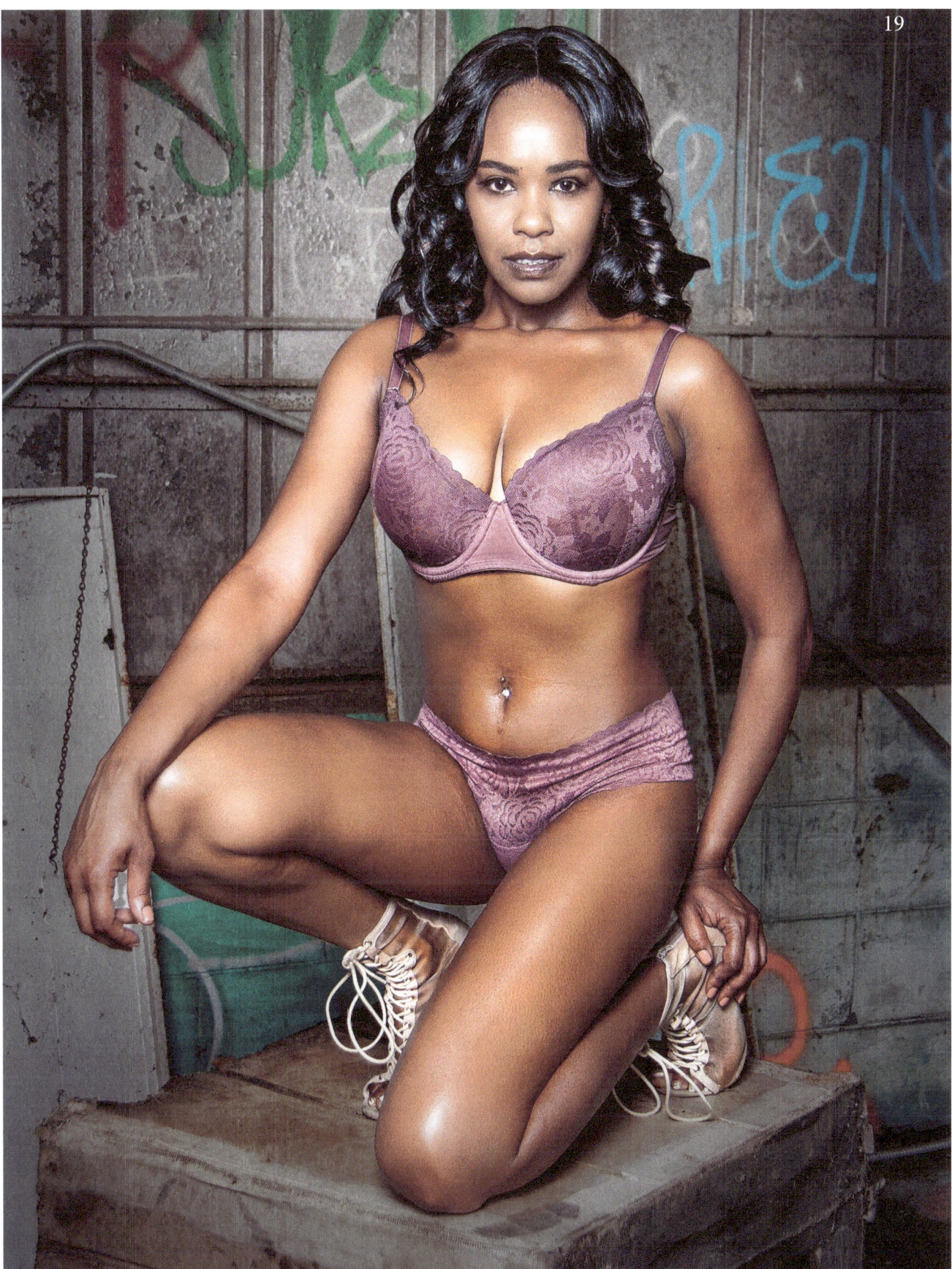

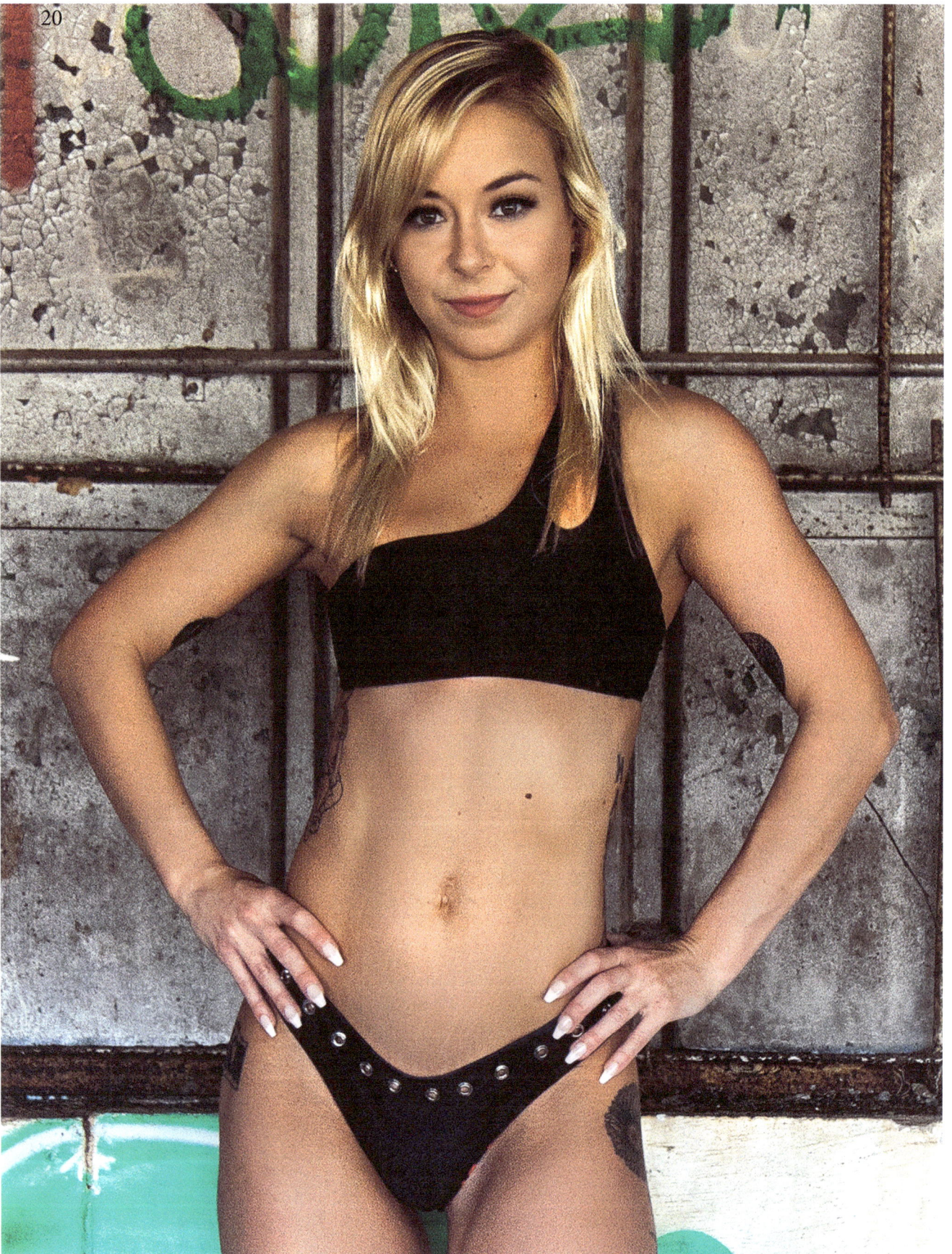

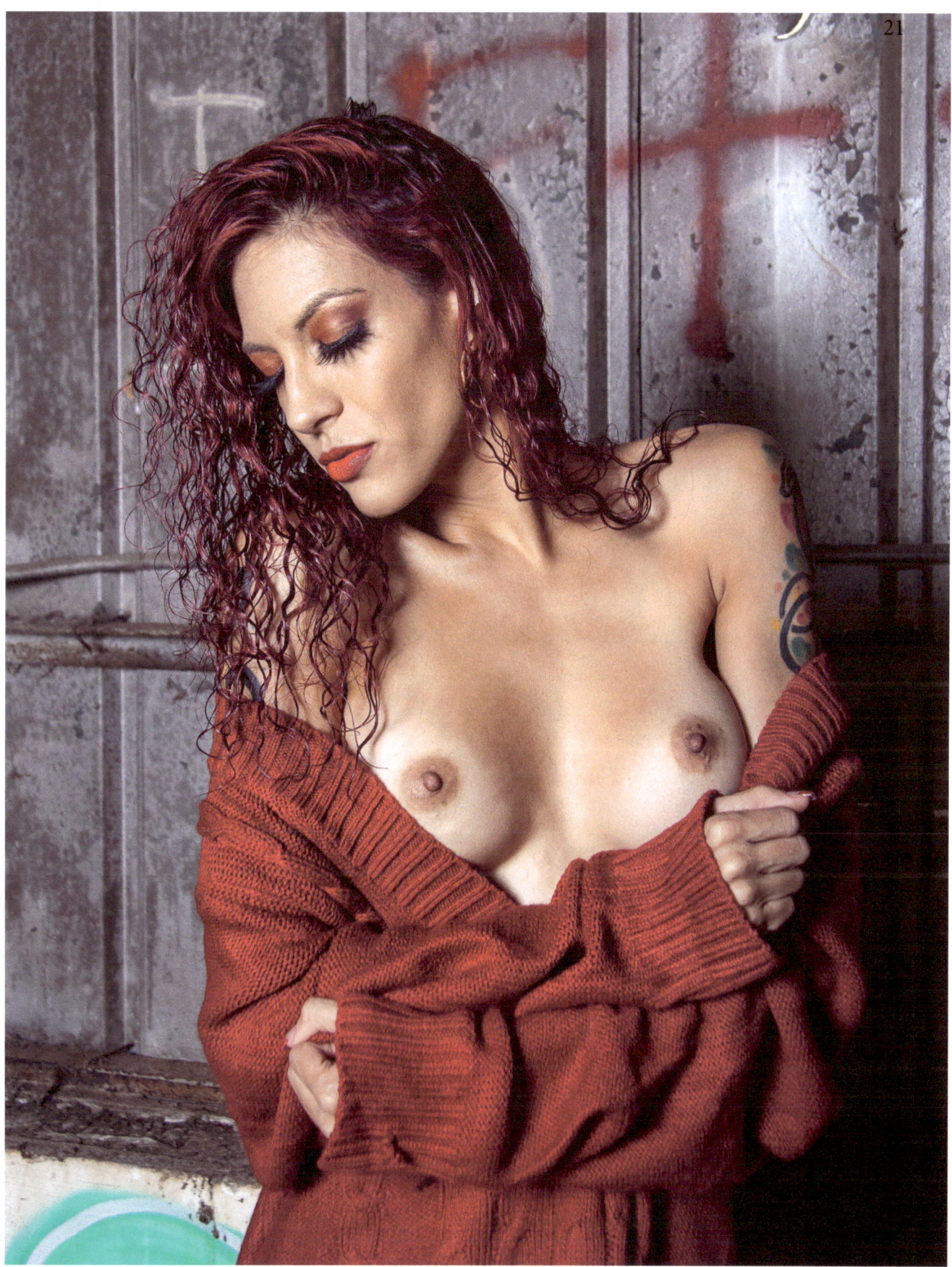

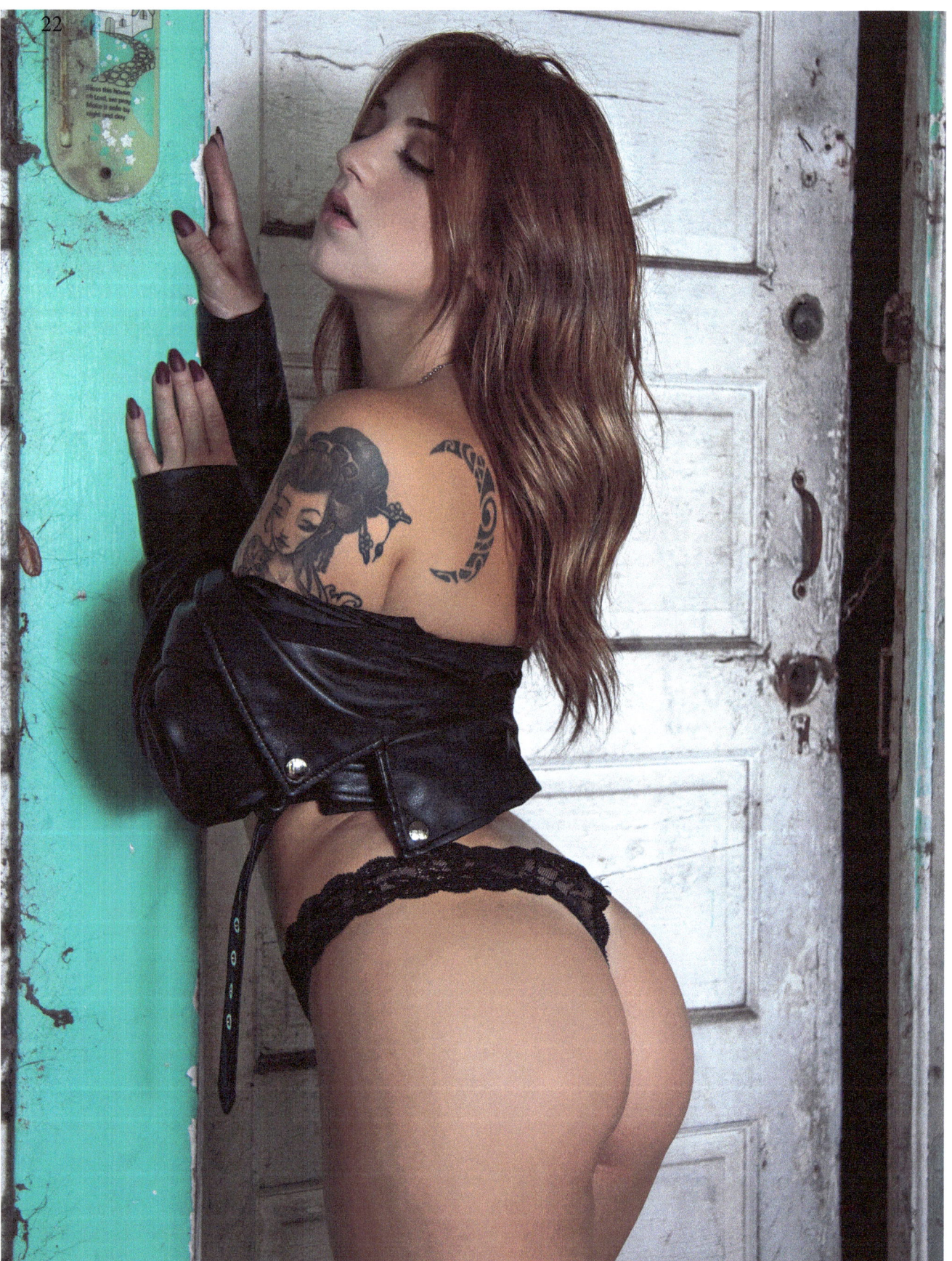

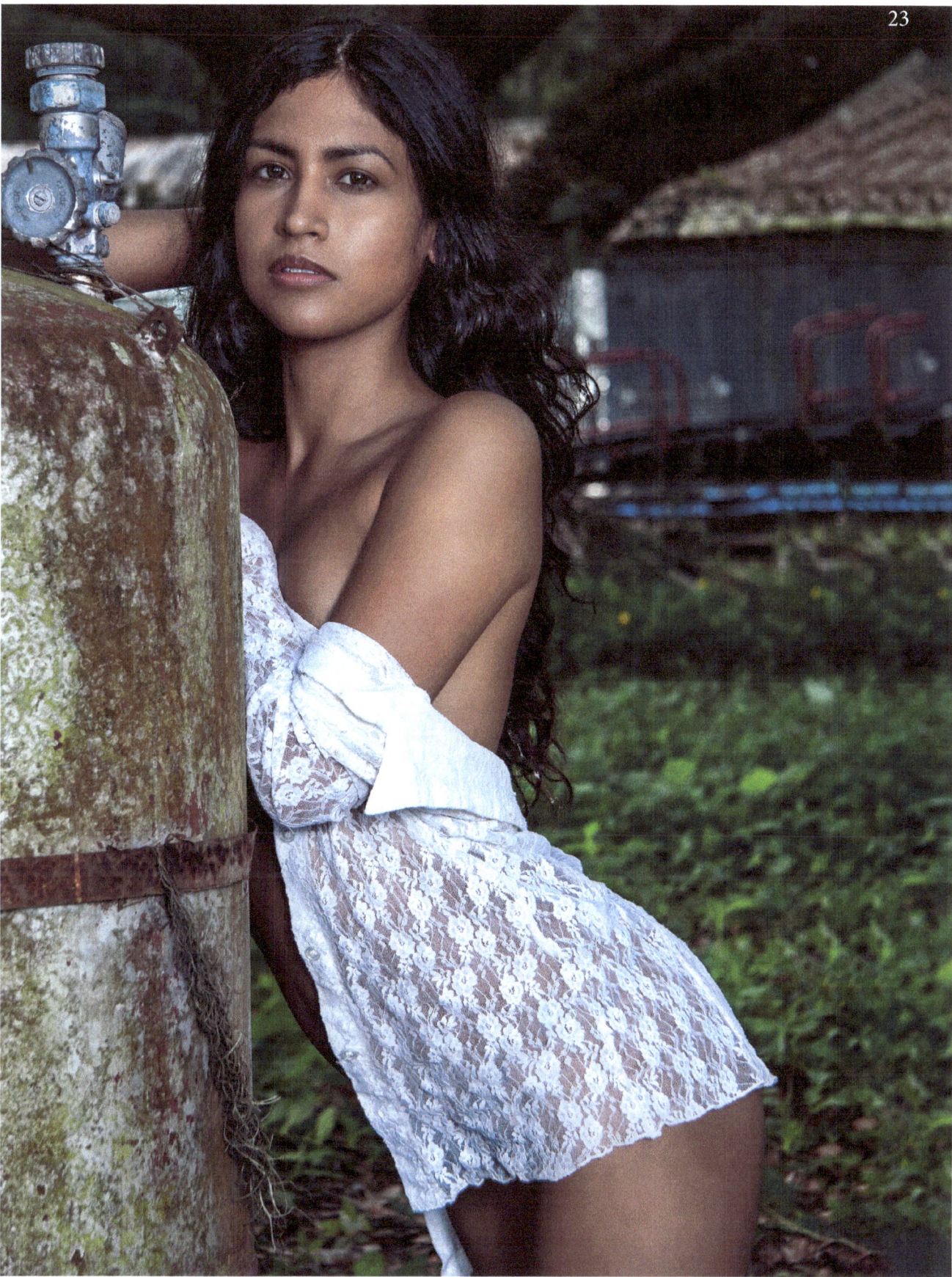

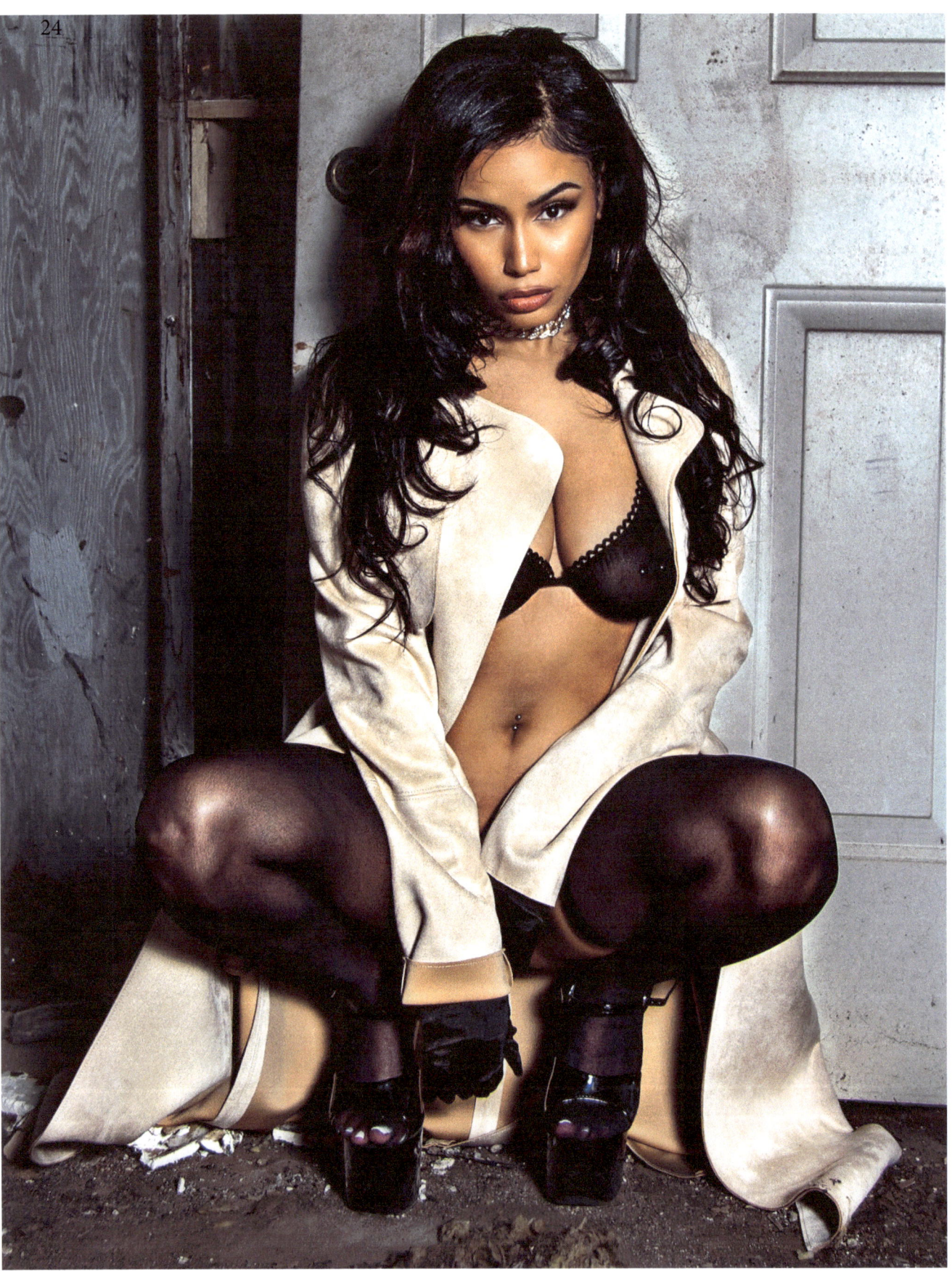

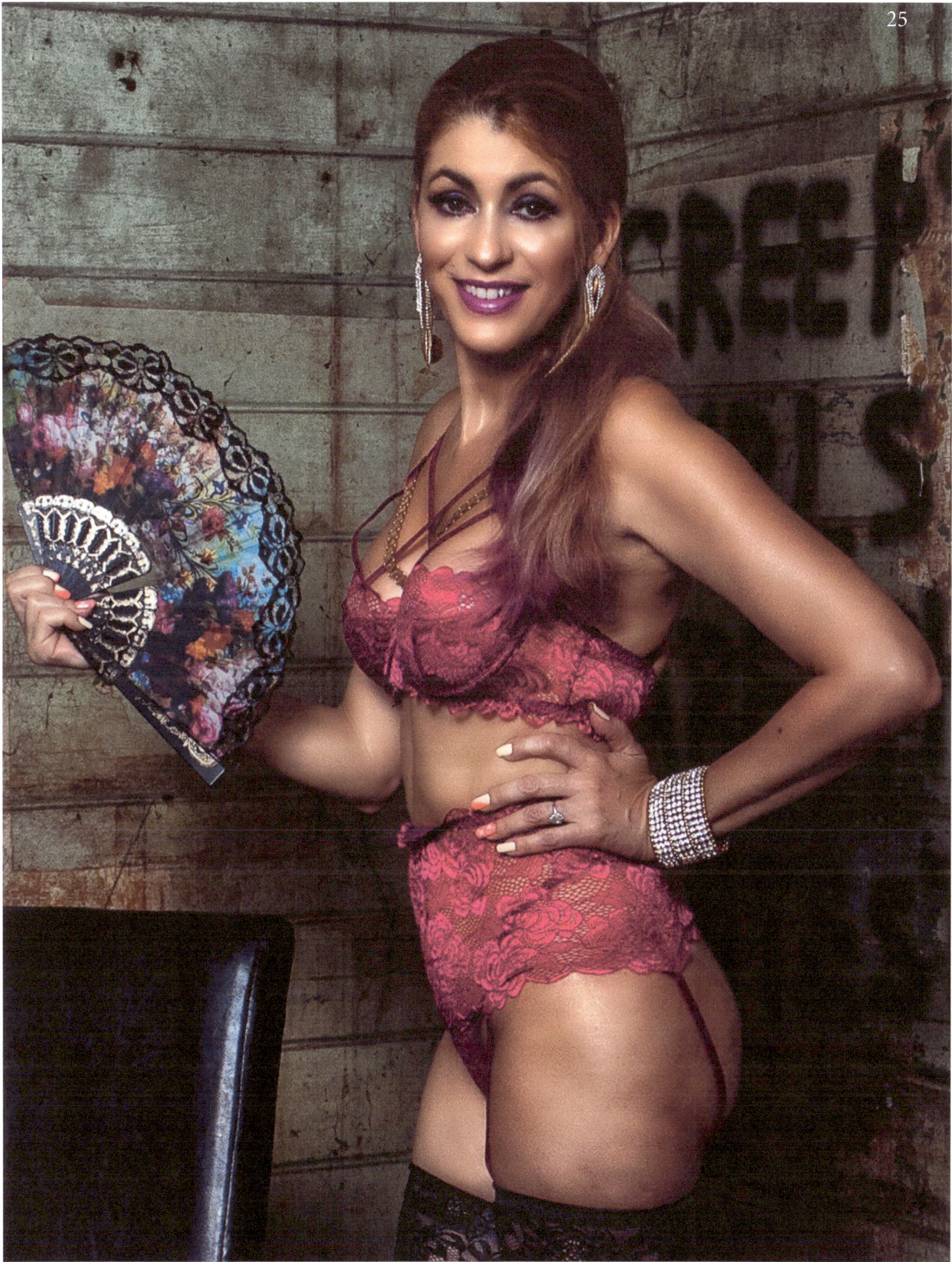

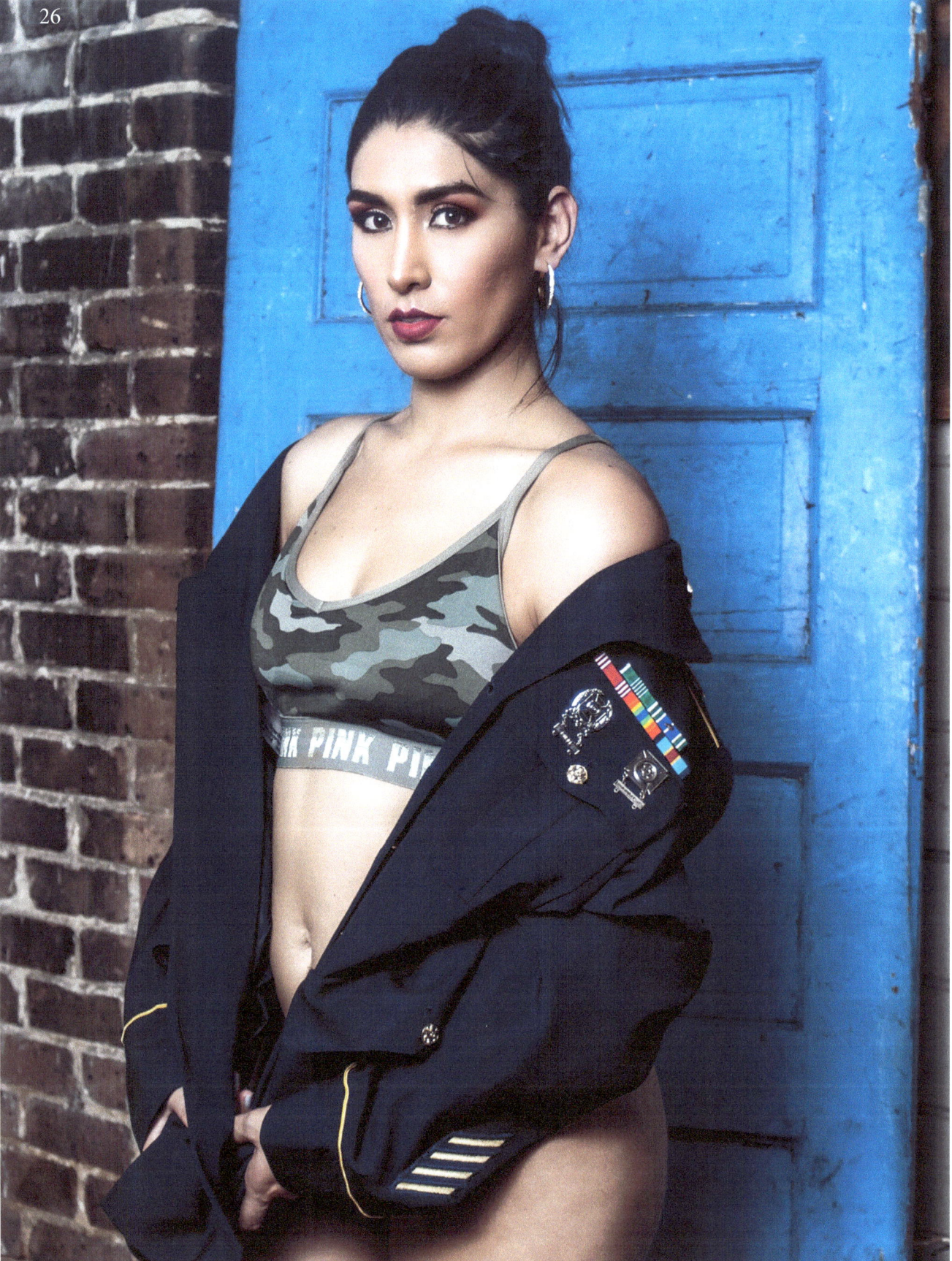

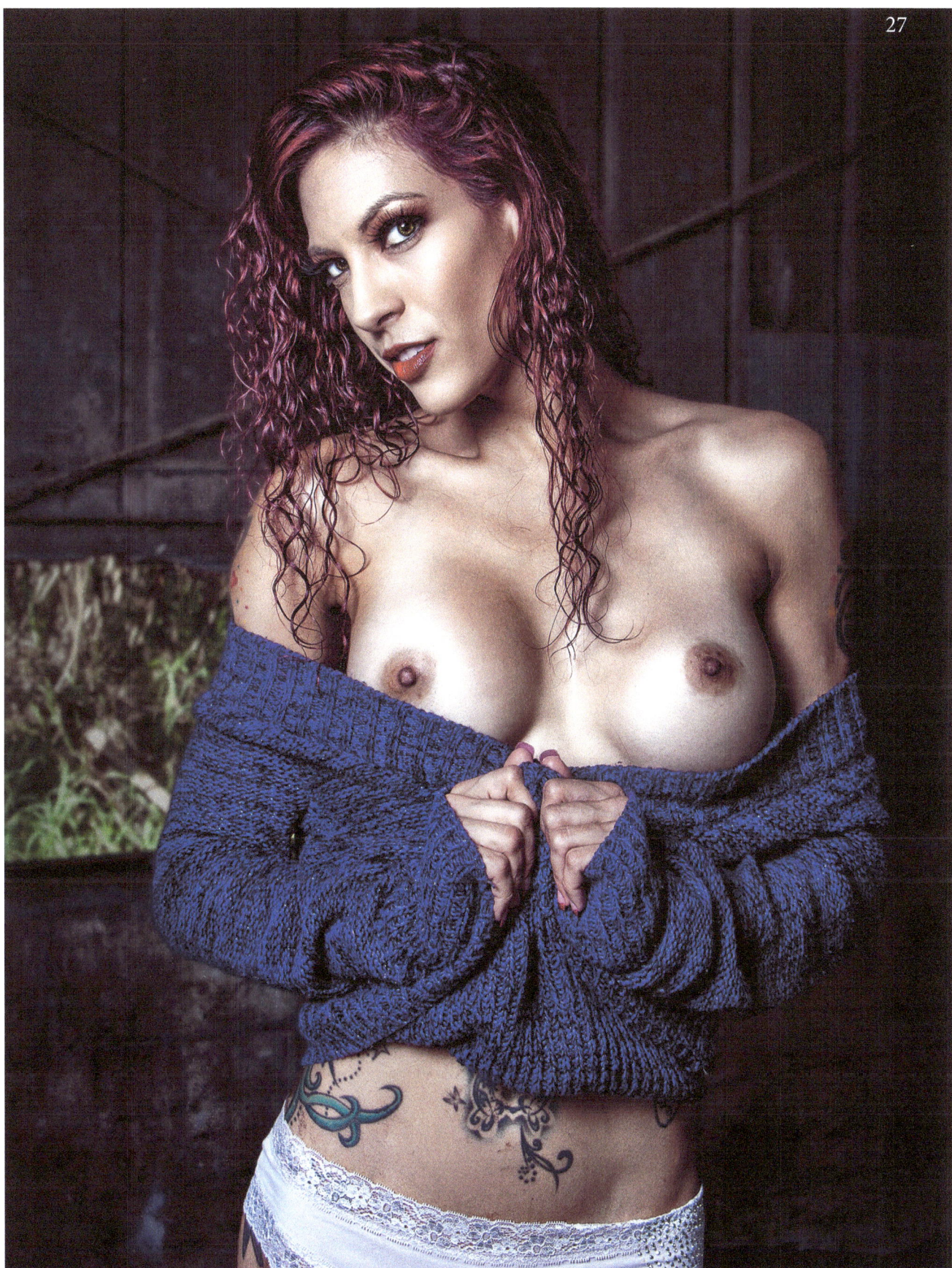

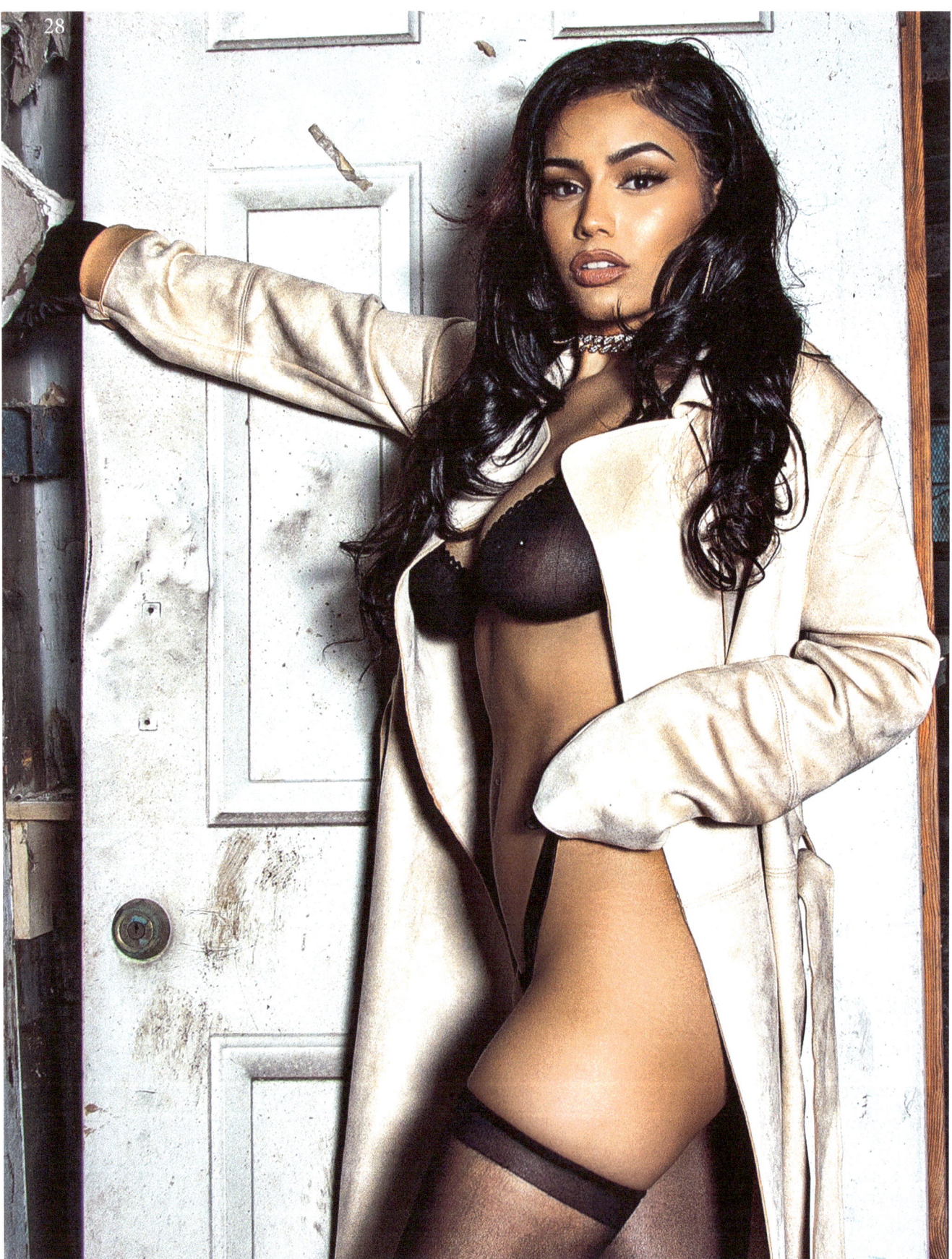

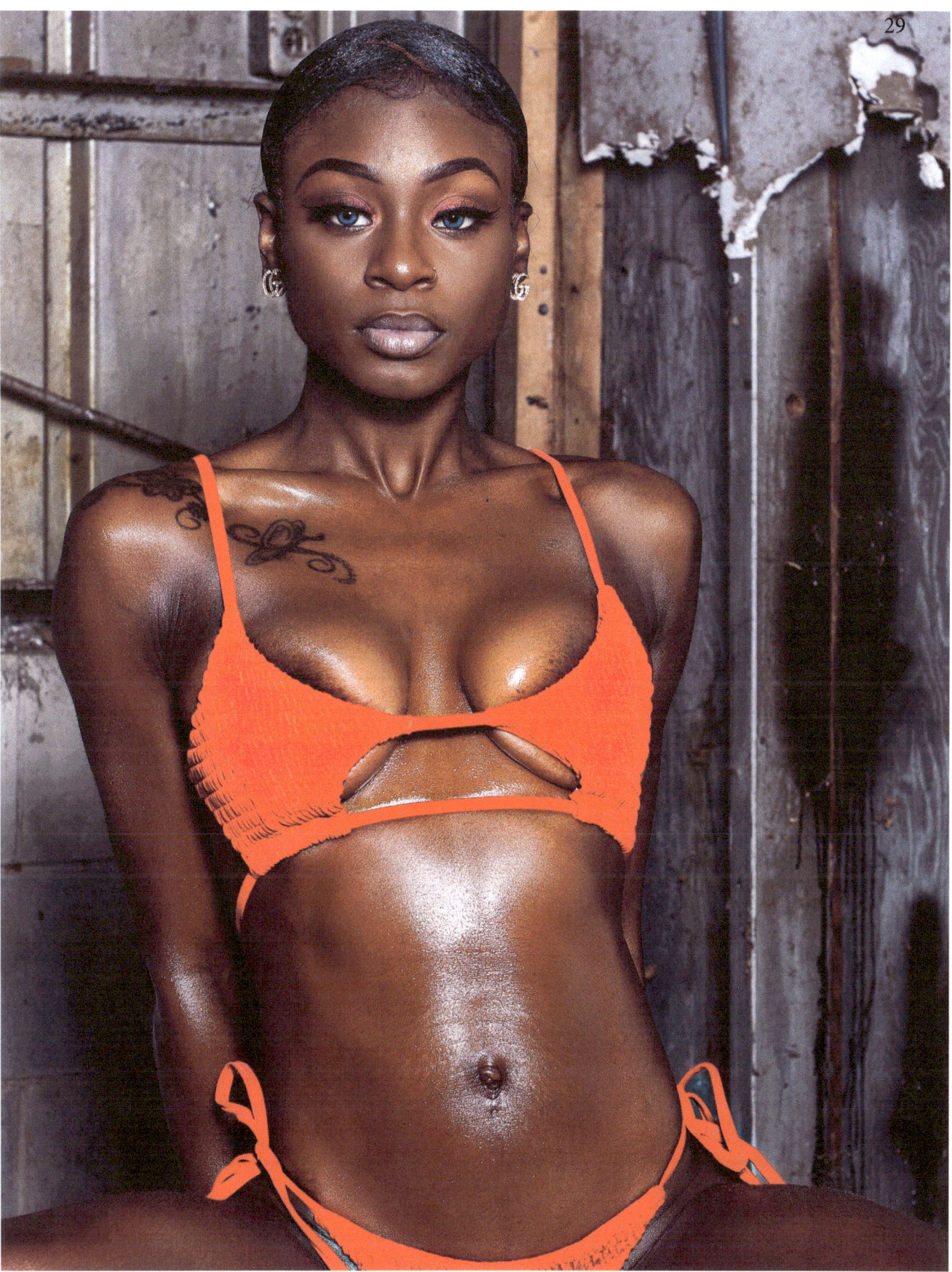

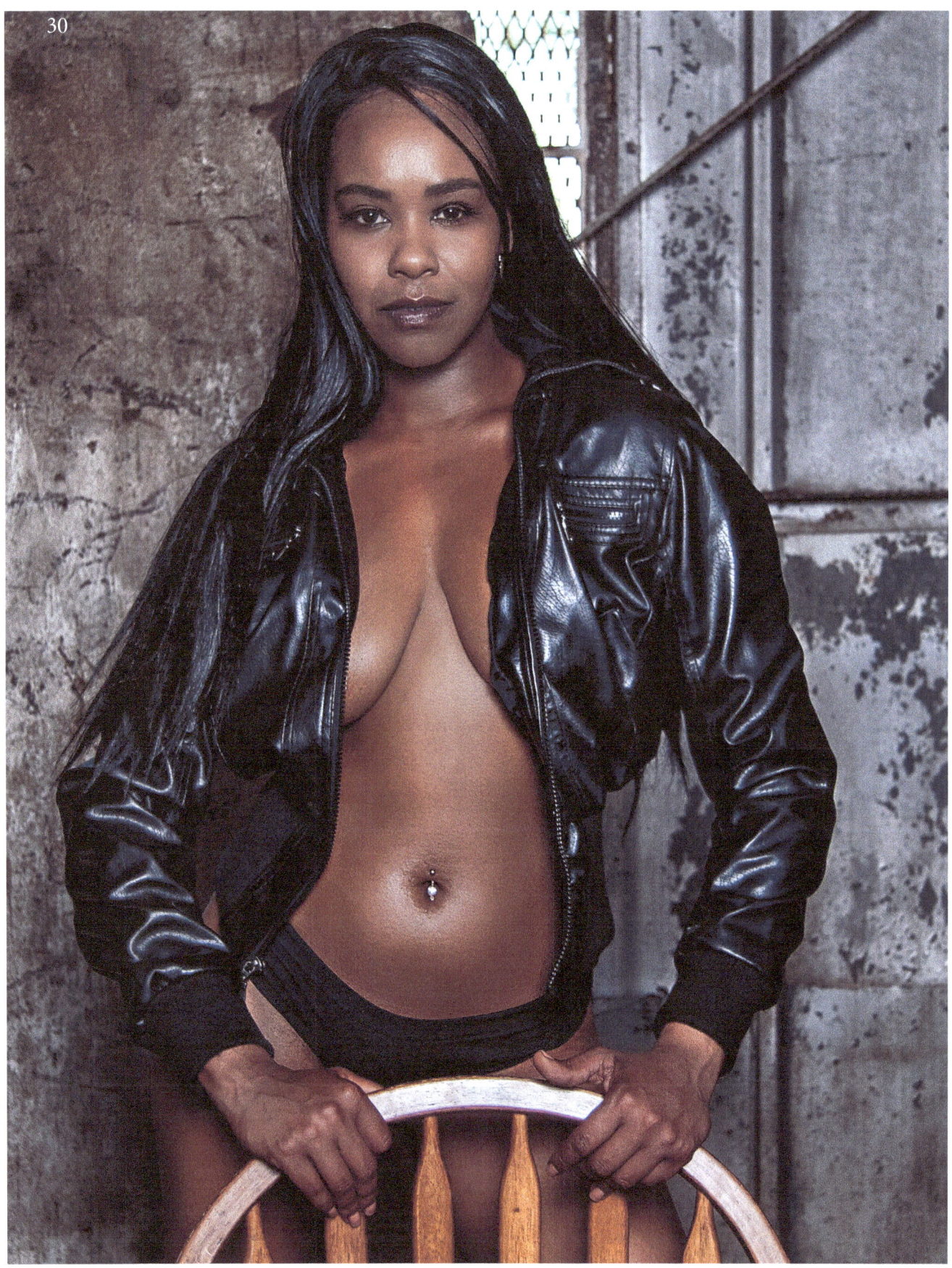

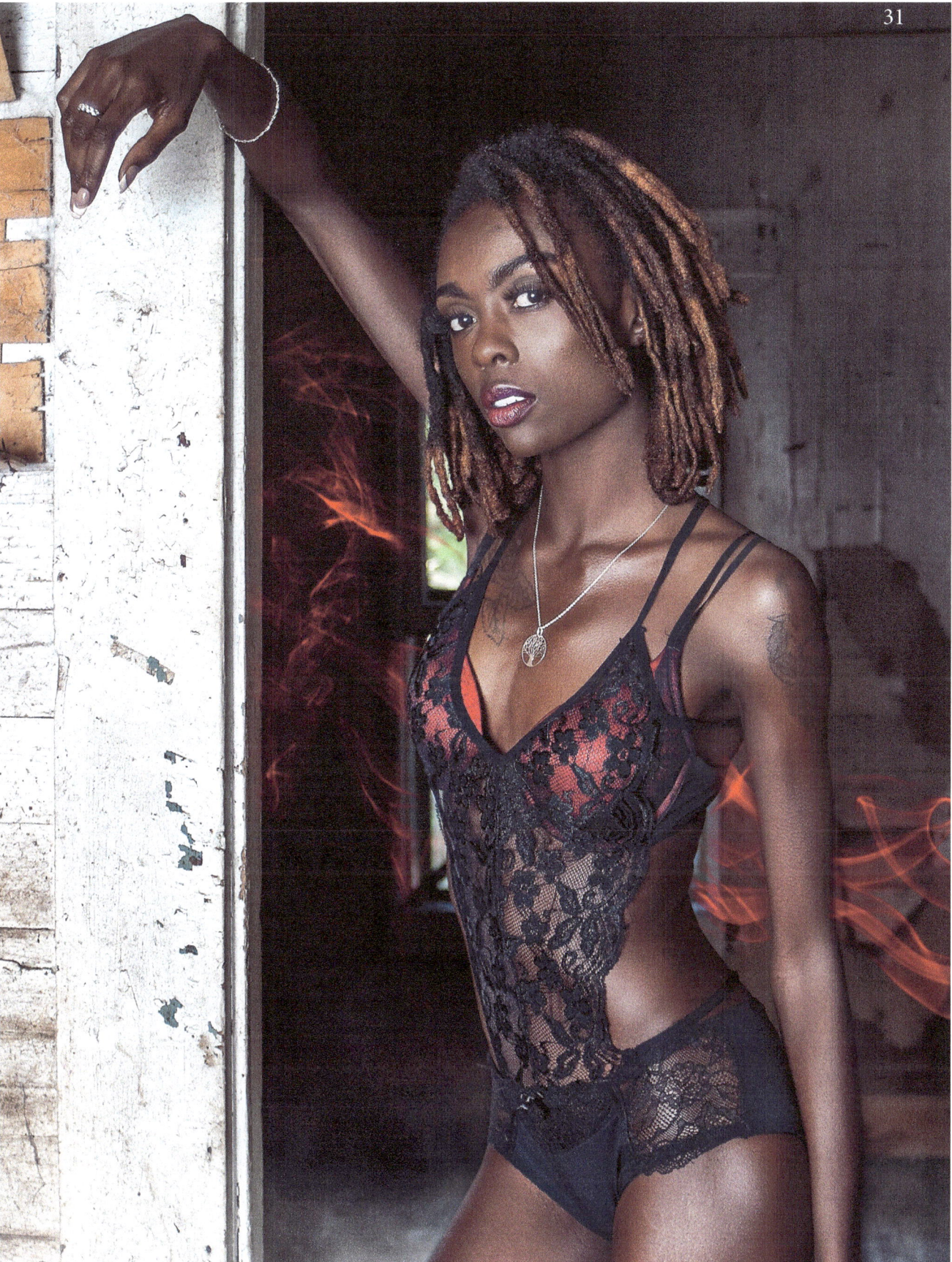

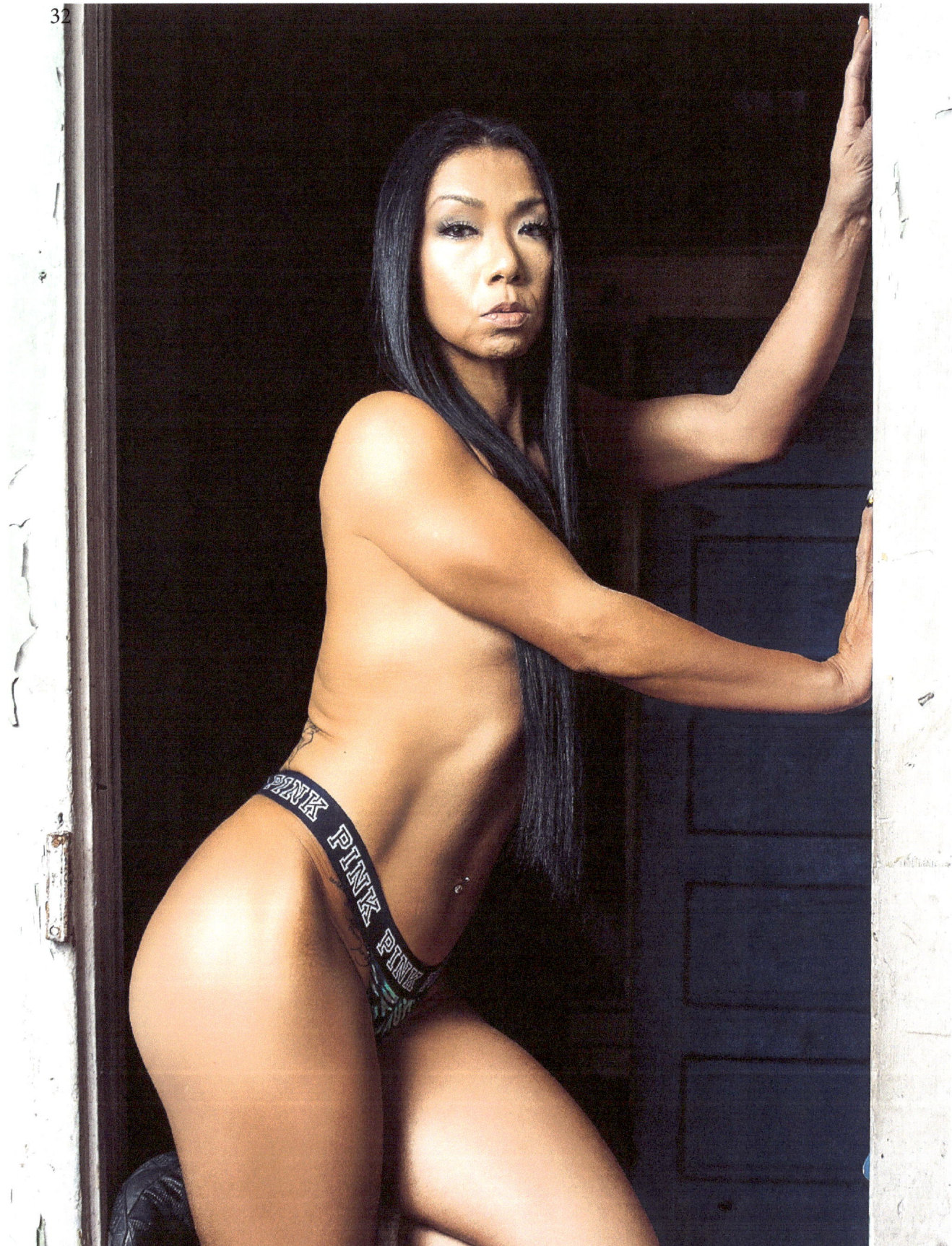

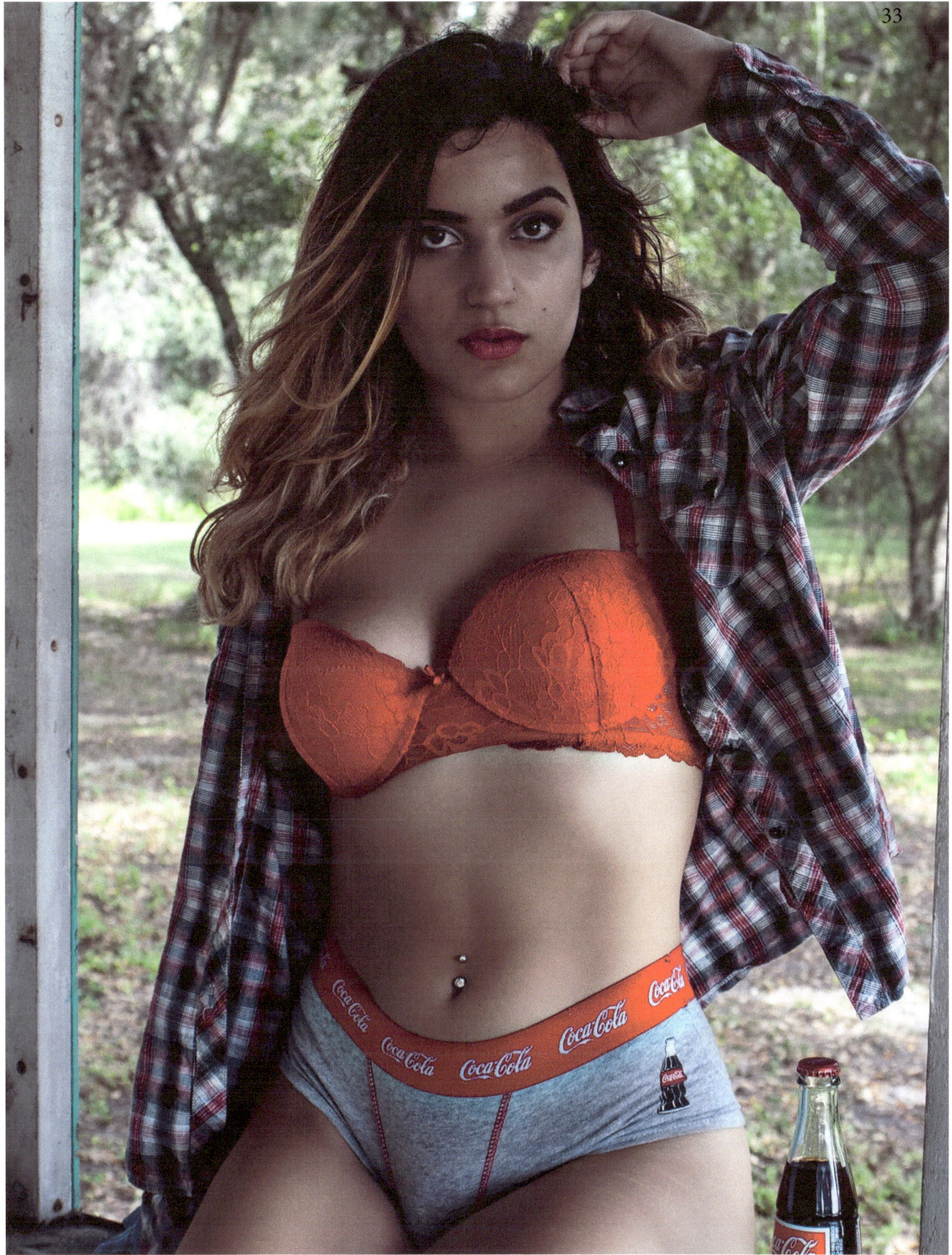

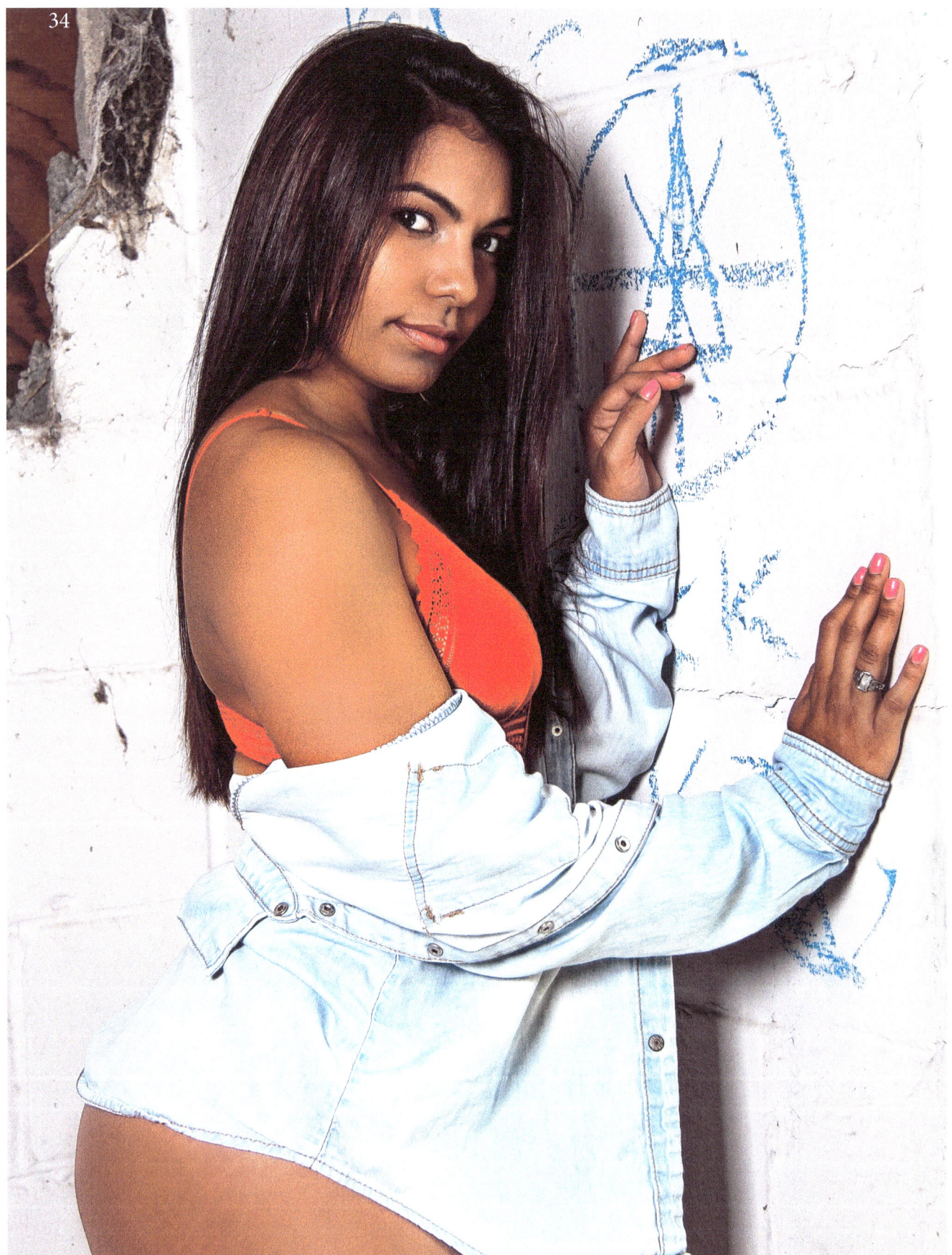

Last Words

By no means am I trying to pretend that I am an accomplished professional in the art of photography. On the contrary, I am just an amateur. The photos in this photo booklet demonstrate the evolution of my abilities as a photographer and as a graphic artist. It's just a hobby, something I like to do.

Over time I have accumulated a certain amount of work material of which I am proud enough to dare to publish in a booklet. As I had already said in one of the previous pages, this booklet is not a publication to show the reader the steps to follow to imitate my style. This booklet is just a collection of some of my work.

I have worked with a large number of models in the state of Florida. Some have traveled from places as far away as Michigan, North Carolina, and even Canada. My style is very easy. I'm not constantly telling the model how to pose. I prefer that they feel free to do what they know that they do good and that that comes out natural and well for them. What they know makes them look beautiful. When a model feels uncomfortable she reflects it in her facial gestures and all these facial gestures are reflected in the photos. I try to be very careful to avoid this.

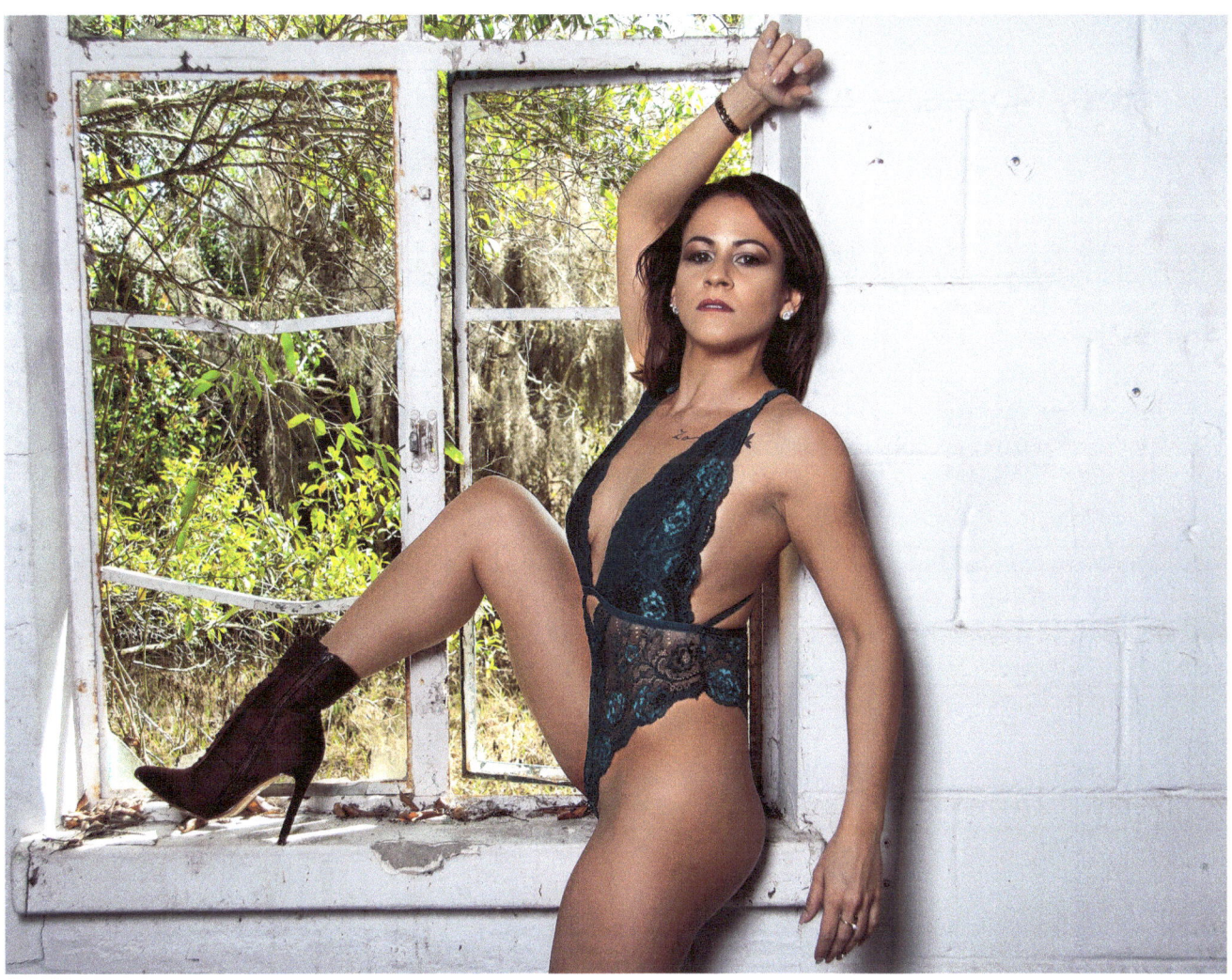

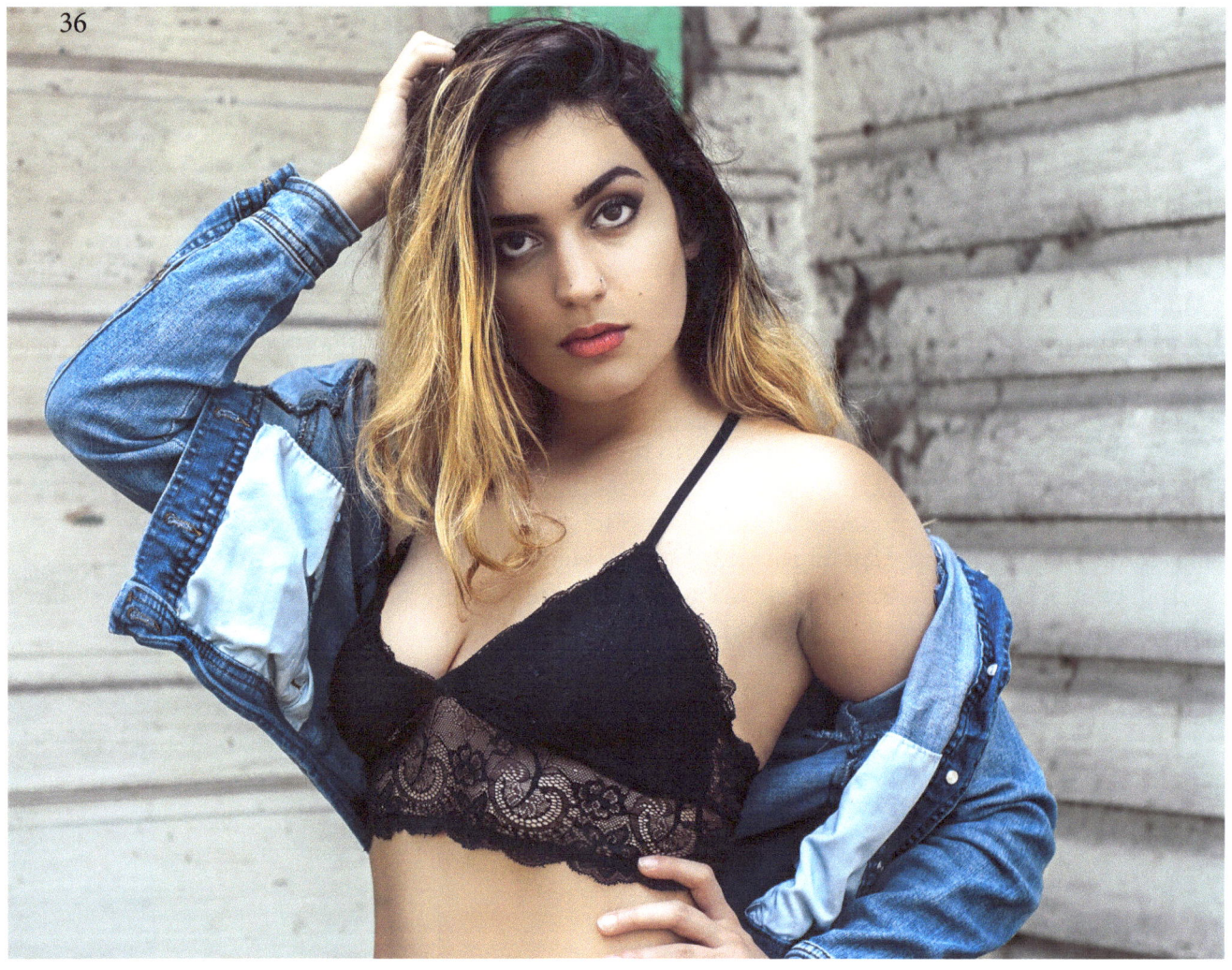

My Canon cameras are not new. Photography is not a source of income for me. I cannot afford new equipment on my regular job income. I think the photographic equipment I have is good enough to produce the result I am looking to create.

Much of my work consists of photos of models in underwear, lingerie, implicit nudity and some provocative nudity. My intention is to create tasteful art. I try very hard to prevent a good artistic photo from being viewed as a vulgar piece of pornography. The models use their bodies to project their art. It is their form of artistic expression. The photographer's job is to capture this medium of expression in a way that can be considered beautiful, attractive, and artistic. That evokes admiration and good feelings.

People have said that my photography and retouching work is refreshing, extraordinary, and beautiful. There are also those who have said that it is vulgar, degrading and even pornographic. I cannot be an impartial judge of my own creations. Please, be the judge.

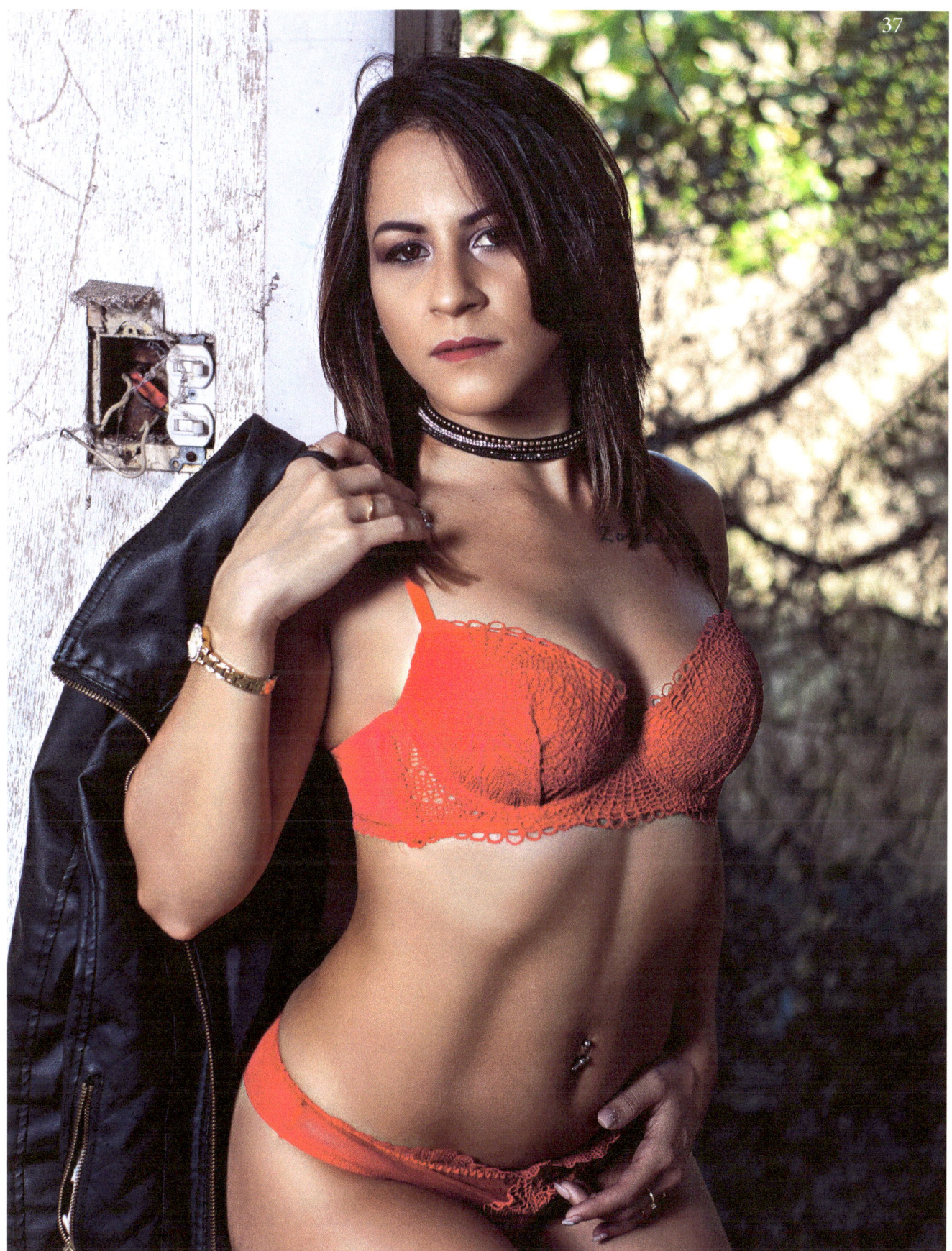

Models

Name	Page	Instagram Handle
Lisa Zuccon Rodriguez	2, 13, 22, cover	@lisamjrodriguez
Tureygua Inaru	5, 14, 23	N/A
Lily Moise	6, 16, 29	@prettyzoe21
Paola Quevedo	7, 26	@paoq_21
Xiomy Molina	8, 25	@xiomy_molina30
Ayumu Hinata	9, 32	@mjscorpion
Alexis Scott	10, 31	@darkskinnedalexis
Tiffany Jones	11, 21, 27	@exoticavixen_model
Rosalie Webb	12, 33, 36	@ro.webb19
Brianna VanCura	15, 24, 28, cover	@itsbriannabltch
Karina Quiñones	17, 35, 37	@model_karinapr_
Solange Marrero	18, 34	@Solange Marrero
Mercedes Cerutti	19, 30	@m.carii
Olivia DeLemos	20	@olivia.delemos

www.ingramcontent.com/pod-product-compliance
Lightning Source LLC
Chambersburg PA
CBHW040452220526
45473CB00004B/1603